AFRICAN EXODUS

AFRICAN EXODUS

Migration and the Future of Europe

Asfa-Wossen Asserate

Translated by Peter Lewis

Introduction by David Goodhart

Published in 2018 by
HAUS PUBLISHING LTD
70 Cadogan Place
London SW1X 9AH

Originally published in German as *Die neue Völkerwanderung: Wer Europa bewahren will, muss Afrika retten* by Asfa-Wossen Asserate
© by Ullstein Buchverlage GmbH, Berlin. Published in 2016 by Propyläen Verlag
Translation Copyright © 2018 by Peter Lewis
Introduction Copyright © 2018 by David Goodhart

The moral rights of the authors have been asserted

A CIP catalogue record for this book is available from the British Library

ISBN: 978-1-910376-90-4
eISBN: 978-1-910376-91-1

Typeset in Garamond by MacGuru Ltd

Printed in Spain

'No one leaves home unless home is the mouth of a shark'
                                    – Warsan Shire, 'Home'

To the millions of African refugees dispersed across all
continents who have been forced to swallow the bitter pill
of exile, I dedicate this book in solidarity and in the fervent
hope that their martyrdom may soon end.
                                    – Asfa-Wossen Asserate

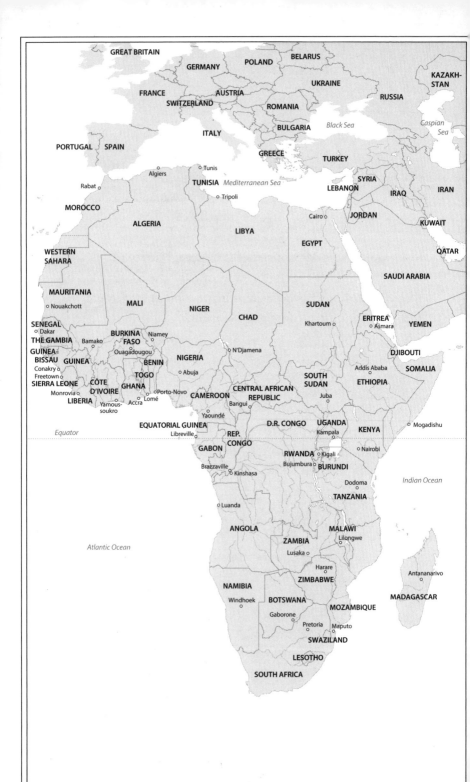

CONTENTS

PROLOGUE

I was a refugee too

I was once a refugee as well; I too have my personal tale of flight. While the revolution took its course in my homeland during the spring and summer of 1974, bringing about the downfall of the Empire of Ethiopia, I was a student in the German city of Frankfurt am Main. From my small student flat, I listened to the radio to follow the events in my home country, which also engulfed my family. First, my father, Prince Asserate Kassa, a leading politician of the empire, was detained by the military junta that now regarded itself as the new government of Ethiopia. Shortly afterwards, my mother and my siblings found themselves in the firing line, as the military took them into custody too. On 24 November 1974 there came a radio report that more than 60 leading politicians of the imperial government had been murdered in Addis Ababa – one of them was my father. No charges had ever been brought against him, nor had he been brought to trial. Like the others, he had simply been taken from the gaol under cover of darkness and summarily executed by firing squad. The atrocity went down in history as Ethiopia's Bloody Saturday.

What this meant for me took some time to sink in. My father was dead. My mother and my siblings were incarcerated without charge – but at least they were still alive. I was the only member of our family who was living freely and safely. A few months later my Ethiopian passport expired. I arranged a meeting at the Ethiopian embassy in Bonn. The ambassador, whom I knew personally, was astonished that I should still be in possession of my passport. He took a few hours to consult with Addis Ababa. Then he announced that a new Ethiopian passport could not be issued to me because of my 'counter-revolutionary activities'. At a stroke, I had become a stateless person.

The following day I applied for asylum in Frankfurt – in those days this was still a very rare occurrence for an Ethiopian. Normally, one would have been required to present oneself in person to the so-called Federal Department for the Recognition of Foreign Refugees, which was located in a small town in Middle Franconia called Zirndorf, but in my case, a decision was reached on the basis of my personal records. It took no more than a week for me to receive a notification that my claim had been accepted, along with a 'foreigner's travel document' that guaranteed me the right of abode and the right to work in Germany for the next seven years.

'Those who are being persecuted politically have the right to asylum,' stipulated Article 16 of the German constitution. I was a textbook case of a political refugee – but judging by today's standards I was far from being a typical refugee. I had not had to use the services of a people-trafficker, paying through the nose to do so. I had not had to travel for days on end through the desert with a backpack containing all my worldly possessions, driven on by the fear of being discovered by the military or the police. I had not had to spend months languishing in a detention camp, stigmatised as an 'illegal alien' and hoping that I might somehow, someday, be allowed to continue my onward journey. I had not had to make a perilous sea voyage crammed together with hundreds of others in an unseaworthy rubber dinghy. I had not been locked into the pitch-black trailer of a lorry, fearful of whether the doors would ever be opened again while I was still alive. I had not had to stand in line outside a government department at five in the morning, day after day for weeks and months on end, just in order to be able to submit my application for asylum. I had not had to spend many anxious months or years condemned to inactivity, living in a hall that had been repurposed as mass refugee accommodation and plagued by uncertainty as to whether I would ultimately be allowed to remain in the country. I had not had to undergo the difficult task of coming to terms with a society whose language and culture were totally alien to me, for I had learnt German as a child at school in Ethiopia and had familiarised myself with German customs and practices as a student.

Back in 1974, I was one of very few asylum seekers. In Frankfurt there was just one other refugee from Ethiopia who had been made stateless; in the whole of Germany there may have been around a dozen or so. Now I am one of many. In the environs of Frankfurt alone, there are 10,000 Ethiopian refugees, and throughout the world there are 2.5 million of us. My story ended well: after seven years as an asylum seeker in Germany I was granted German citizenship, and I think I have thoroughly integrated myself into German society. I was lucky – something I repeat to myself every morning in great gratitude as a kind of mantra.

Nowadays, as we read daily reports of the streams of people who are on the run worldwide, and as we see the images of the convoys of pick-up trucks laden with people crossing the Sahara, we should always keep in mind one thing: each and every one of these people is an individual with his or her own destiny; with fears and hopes for a better and more secure future; and with the desire to someday be able, after having found a new life, to look back on the time when he or she was fleeing as a refugee and say, just as I did, 'I was lucky'.

Asfa-Wossen Asserate
Frankfurt am Main, December 2017

INTRODUCTION

By David Goodhart

This is an angry book with plenty to be angry about. When the author, Asfa-Wossen Asserate, claimed asylum in Germany in 1974 after the coup in Ethiopia, in which his politician father was murdered, there were only a dozen Ethiopians in the whole country. There are now about 10,000 in the Frankfurt area alone, where he lives.

The number of Africans trying to leave their countries to build a better life in the West is estimated at more than 1 million each year, excluding those fleeing war or natural disasters.

Why are they coming, or wanting to come, in such large numbers? Because too many African countries are not offering a future. Ethiopia itself produces about 35,000 graduates every year but only around 5 per cent find paid employment in the country. As Asserate says, if you take a room at the Sheraton Hotel in Addis Ababa the likelihood is the that maid who serves you coffee will have a bachelor's degree to her name.

Many of the refugees who set out to Europe are from the middle class, just the people who should be building Africa's future. Their reason for leaving is no mystery as Asserate explains with great force and clarity: it is the result of how many of the 54 African countries are governed. Both politics and business in Africa are too often extractive, rent-seeking activities, a zero-sum game designed for places with little tradition of social trust or cooperation.

Western countries work because the state is neither too strong nor too weak. In Africa it is usually both too strong and too weak. Too strong in the sense that many leaders still flout the rule of law with impunity, crushing their opponents or casually disregarding constitutional safeguards. Too weak in the sense that many countries do not provide the basics in which people and businesses can flourish: the rule of law, social peace, decent infrastructure and adequate health and education.

The introduction of multi-party elections in the 1990s in many more African states was considered a great breakthrough. No more. African governments have become skilled at manipulating and subverting elections. Moreover, the first past the post electoral system is blamed for fomenting ethnic rivalries in countries like Kenya, Ethiopia, Nigeria and Uganda.

The history of colonialism of course twisted Africa's politics and economics out of shape. It was responsible for creating artificial entities with no consensus between groups, and economies based mainly on raw material extraction.

But blaming colonialism will not do any longer. Africa has had more than 50 years in most cases to create viable democracies and economies that do more than depend on the continent's immense raw material wealth, remittances and Western aid.

In a few places (Botswana is usually cited as the golden boy) it is doing just that. But overall Africa remains a confusing picture of promise and dynamism alongside grinding poverty and abuse of power. Six of the 10 most fragile states in the world are in Africa: Somalia, South Sudan, the Central African Republic, Sudan, Chad and the Democratic Republic of Congo. And according to Transparency International 14 of the 25 most corrupt countries in the world are in Africa (and that doesn't even include Nigeria).

Nearly half of Africa's population south of the Sahara still live below the World Bank poverty line. And perhaps the most depressing statistic of all in a book full of them: over the last 40 years Nigeria has earned more than $400 billion from oil exports yet over the same period the number of Nigerians living on less than $1 a day grew from 19 million to 90 million. And rich Nigerians still invariably travel abroad for medical operations, not trusting their own health services.

For every promising development such as the mobile telephony revolution, there are wrong turns or historic blights: the current craze for selling huge tracts of farmland to foreigners or the curse of rapid population growth. Only 30 per cent of married women use contraception and large families are still seen as an old age insurance policy in rural Africa. The population of 1.2 billion is expected to double by 2050.

Yet Africa continues to haemorrhage its educated young. As the author Ivan Krastev has observed: 'The spread of the internet has made it possible for young Africans to see with one click of a mouse how Europeans live. People no longer compare their lives with those of their neighbours but with the planet's most prosperous inhabitants. They dream not of the future but of other places.'

Europe bears a share of responsibility for current African failures, whether in providing a safe haven for the financial proceeds of corruption or excluding African textiles and agricultural produce while dumping its own subsidised agricultural produce on Africans. Asserate tells the appalling story of how cheap tomato paste from the EU destroyed indigenous tomato farmers in Ghana, some of whom ended up as illegal immigrant tomato pickers in Apulia in Italy, helping to produce the very paste that destroyed their livelihoods.

Europe even colludes in the 'brain drain' sucking in the

educated people from African countries that can ill afford to lose them. (There are said to be more Zimbabwean doctors and nurses in London than in Zimbabwe.) We are always implored to think of a refugee as an individual with hopes and aspirations but we should also remember that in many cases they are the skilled and dynamic people who should be leading both political and economic reform in the societies they come from.

Europe should continue to discourage the illegal, and sometimes fatal, flows across the Mediterranean and even send back those who have tried to enter through the back door. At the same time Africa's educated young must be given greater legal avenues to study and work in the West *temporarily*.

Western publics will not accept the rapid demographic change that goes with persistent large-scale immigration, yet for both moral and economic reasons rich countries should remain open to flows of the talented young from developing countries. The way to square this circle and to benefit both rich and poor countries is to make almost all this immigration temporary.

Rich countries, especially those like Britain and France with colonial responsibilities in Africa, should channel some of their development aid into mass scholarship programmes for African countries. The rising middle class can thereby feel a connection to the West but bring back their experience and knowledge to develop their own societies.

'Africa,' as Barack Obama memorably said, 'doesn't need strongmen, it needs strong institutions.' And, he might have added, it will not be saved by Europe's 'saviour complex'. A country cannot be developed from the outside, in the words of the British-American economist Angus Deaton.

There are always promising developments in Africa: most recently in both Zimbabwe and South Africa. And even

Asserate's Ethiopia is having some success breaking into global industrial markets. It is doing this by clustering firms near an airport, ensuring good logistics and reliable, affordable electricity – not complicated but all too rare in Africa.

If these trends are to bear fruit it will be through self-help allied to intelligent support from the West. More than $1 trillion of aid over the past 50 years must be largely regarded as a failure. Too much of it, like much of Chinese investment today, has helped to reinforce a rotten political status quo and so has been a form of anti-development aid. Africa's most progressive new leaders, like Ghana's president Nana Addo Dankwa Akufo-Addo, now talk about 'Ghana beyond aid'.

Unfashionably, Asserate concludes that economic salvation will not come in the medium term from industrialisation but from better support for small- and medium-sized farms. That in turn requires an end to Europe's harmful trade policies.

But for Asserate good governance is the Alpha and Omega of African progress and Europe must support such progress by linking aid, and more Africa-friendly trade arrangements, far more rigorously to political progress. And the battle against Islamic fundamentalism must not be allowed to divert from this goal in the same way that the Cold War gave too many reactionary regimes a free pass.

Linking aid to politics in this way will, of course, attract accusations of neocolonialism. But to make amends for actual colonialism, which really did undermine African political structures, Europe must risk upsetting the status quo in many places. As Asserate concludes: the only viable way of stopping the human flow out of Africa is for the West to more openly and consciously ally itself with Africa's young reformers.

1

ON THE RUN

The world is out of joint. 65.3 million people are on the run. Bloody conflicts and the fear of persecution have driven them from their homelands. According to a report issued by the United Nations High Commissioner for Refugees (UNHCR) in the summer of 2017, this affects every 113th person on Earth. And with every day that passes, another 34,000 people who fear for their lives leave their homes – at a rate of 24 per minute.[1] A comparison with preceding years shows how dramatic the situation has become. In 2010, the corresponding figure was just 10,900 refugees per day, but by 2012 this had already risen to 21,400. And there is nothing to indicate that the numbers will decline – quite the contrary. Some 12.4 million people were added to the figure in 2015 alone. For the most part, those affected are children and young people. Over half of the refugees are under 18 years of age.

Currently, there are some 65 million refugees throughout the world – roughly the equivalent of the population of France. If all the refugees were brought together in a single country, it would rank in 21st place among the world's most populous nations. However, not all refugees have left their homelands: at the end of 2015, almost two-thirds, or around 40.8 million, were still living within the borders of their home country, while 21.3 million had sought refuge in foreign countries. A further

3.2 million were waiting in foreign countries for their asylum applications to be decided.

The dreadful scenes of the civil wars in Syria, Afghanistan and Iraq have dominated international headlines in recent months and years, but the refugee crisis has long ceased to be confined to the Near East. On the 2015 list of countries from which the most refugees were coming, ranking in third place after Syria and Afghanistan was an African country, Somalia. In the whole of Africa, according to the UNHCR, some 4.4 million people are now on the run – 20 per cent more than the year before.

'We are facing the greatest refugee crisis of our age,' declared United Nations (UN) Secretary-General Ban Ki-Moon. 'But this is not a crisis of numbers, it is a crisis of solidarity.'[2] In Europe, the migration crisis was largely regarded as somebody else's problem, and the daily television images seemed far away – that is, until 2015, when the refugees were suddenly at the gates of Europe. Since then, more than a million people have found their way by boat across the Mediterranean or on foot via the so-called Balkan Route. In Europe, the world's richest continent, they are hoping to find a secure future for themselves and their families.

Yet people do not leave their homelands only because of personal persecution, human rights abuses or extreme violence. Poverty and hunger also drive people to seek a better life elsewhere. In 2015, there were over 244 million migrants worldwide – over 41 per cent more than in 2000.[3] There has long been talk of a new global process of mass migration of people.

Homo migrans

When we hear the term 'mass migration of people' we think, above all, of the historical era of Late Antiquity. The period from the late fourth to the sixth century AD was an 'epoch of mass migration'. It began with the overthrow of the empire of the Ostrogoths by the Huns on the Dnieper River in the year 375, and ended with the Lombard invasion of Italy in the year 568. Over the course of this vast upheaval, peoples such as the Celts, the Teutons and the Slavs moved west and occupied the Mediterranean region, ultimately bringing about the downfall of the Western Roman Empire. However, even the most cursory study of history indicates that there have always been mass migrations and movements of peoples. Indeed, the whole of human history could be said to be one of migration movements.

It is well known that the cradle of all human civilisation is Africa. In 1974, American palaeontologists working in the Afar region of northern Ethiopia came across the remains of what was at that time the oldest bipedal hominid. This fossil find was dated to around 3.2 million years earlier. Because the skeleton was thought to be that of a female, the researchers dubbed it Lucy; in Ethiopia, however, the name given to it was Dinknesh, Amharic for 'you marvel'. In 1992, at an archaeological dig not far away, a relative of Dinknesh was discovered, and was thought to be some 4.4 million years old; in 2001, also in the Afar region, a team led by the Ethiopian palaeontologist Yohannes Haile-Selassie found the skeleton of an even older bipedal hominid – this one almost 6 million years old.

Around 200,000 years ago the ancestors of Dinknesh evolved into our species, which we have given the name *Homo sapiens*. The earliest humans were nomads; around a million years ago they began to leave their original homelands in

Ethiopia, Northern Kenya and Somalia and embark on migratory journeys. Over the course of millennia, they spread throughout the African continent – and ultimately throughout the entire globe. Around 100,000 years ago the first humans left Africa, but it is only some 40,000 years ago that the first of them reached Europe. They adapted themselves to the different climatic conditions found in various parts of the world and evolved their own regional characteristics. Even if many Europeans nowadays might choose to forget it, or are ignorant of the fact in the first place, their evolutionary heritage lies without exception in African migration.

In a process of constant exchange and dialogue between the different cultures, humanity evolved. Accordingly, our species could just as justifiably be given the scientific binomial *Homo migrans* ('itinerant man'). Traces of these historical migrations can be found all around the world. Some 1,500 years ago, African tribes and peoples spread out from West Africa to occupy the east and the south and, interbreeding with the populaces already resident there, went on to settle the whole of Sub-Saharan Africa. The Tutsi, for example, who live in present-day Rwanda, are the descendants of a nomadic people from my home country of Ethiopia. They migrated down the bank of the White Nile in search of pasturage for their animals before finally settling in the 'Land of a Thousand Hills'.

With the discovery and conquest of the Americas by Spanish and Portuguese seafarers in the late fifteenth and early sixteenth centuries, the exchange of goods, plants, animals and humans gained a new dimension. The beginning of the Early Modern period also marked the start of the era of globalisation. European immigrants set about settling the 'New World'. Before long, it was not just goods being traded but people. Between 1519 and 1867, some 9.5 million Africans, predominantly from

West Africa and the west of Central Africa from Senegal down to Angola, were transported to North, Central and South America. They were sold as slaves in exchange for textiles, weapons, salt, horses, alcohol or tobacco.

During the eighteenth and nineteenth centuries, more and more people in Europe began to migrate in an attempt to improve their living conditions. In particular, during the late Industrial Revolution, between the end of the nineteenth century and the outbreak of the First World War, more than 50 million Europeans emigrated to America. Economic crises and starvation caused them to lose hope of ever improving their lot if they remained in their countries of birth; the land of boundless opportunities promised them a better life – yet anyone who made it onto an emigrant ship bound for the Americas was heading toward an uncertain future. In the days before the advent of steam navigation, a transatlantic crossing could, depending on the prevailing winds and sea conditions, last for up to 10 weeks. The sanitary conditions on board were often appalling. Most passengers made the crossing in 'steerage' class, crammed below decks with an absolute minimum of space, in conditions of virtually no natural light. And when the migrants arrived at the port of New York, full of uncertainty and expectation, they were greeted scarcely more warmly than African and Middle Eastern refugees arriving in Europe are nowadays. The writer Robert Louis Stevenson, who himself embarked on an emigrant ship sailing from Liverpool to New York in 1879, stated: 'Emigration, from a word of the most cheerful import, came to sound most dismally in my ear. There is nothing more agreeable to picture and nothing more pathetic to behold.'[4] No doubt Stevenson's sentiment would find echoes of assent in many of today's migrants who have set off on such an odyssey.

Who are refugees?

Migration takes, and has always taken, the most diverse range of forms.[5] It can be a voluntary action, such as moving abroad to further one's education or for work: a person might move to another country to take up a position there, to attend a university, or to gain further vocational qualifications. Many a person finds him- or herself impelled to travel abroad for love (migration researchers refer to such instances as 'marriage migration'), whereas others simply feel drawn to a particular city or culture ('cultural migration') or by the pleasant climate of a particular location ('lifestyle migration', which is especially prevalent among older, retired people). However, frequently there is an element of coercion to migration, as is the case with slavery and people-trafficking, or deportation and forcible expulsion. The term 'coercive migration' also encompasses instances where people are forced to leave their home country on political, ethno-nationalistic, racist or religious grounds; on the grounds of sexual identity; or because of a catastrophe (either a natural disaster or one brought about by human agency).

For all those who attempt to escape a danger that threatens their very existence, and who as a result turn their back on their homeland, the word 'refugee' has established itself as a catch-all term. The 1951 Refugee Convention – which was agreed in Geneva just a few years after the end of the Second World War, and reworked in 1967 – provides a definition of a refugee:

> [A person who] owing to a well-founded fear of being persecuted for reasons of race, religion, nationality, membership of a particular social group or political opinion, is outside the country of his nationality and is unable or, owing to such fear, is unwilling to avail himself of the protection of that country; or who, not having a nationality and being outside

the country of his former habitual residence as a result of such events, is unable or, owing to such fear, is unwilling to return to it.[6]

Worldwide, 147 states have now adopted this convention, which guarantees anyone meeting the stipulated criteria a legal status that is binding in international law. This ensures them protection from discrimination due to race, religion or country of origin; religious freedom; immunity from prosecution for illegal entry; protection from deportation; free access to courts; and the issuing of a passport. However, the 1951 Refugee Convention also has its blind spots: internal refugees, who are displaced within their own country, are not covered by the agreement. Likewise, people who flee across borders from war or other conflict situations do not necessarily enjoy its protection unless they can demonstrate that at least one of the named grounds for becoming a refugee pertains in their case. And the many people who flee to escape life-threatening economic hardship have no claim to special protection. Furthermore, gender-specific persecution is not mentioned, and nor are those people who flee their homelands as a result of environmental and natural disasters. It is also true that, while the 1951 Refugee Convention guarantees a person protected status, it does not grant them an automatic right to asylum. It is left to individual countries to regulate this, and even within the European Union each member state follows its own self-imposed provisions.

One factor distinguishes the movements of refugees and other migrants in former times from those taking place nowadays. Formerly, people would emigrate to areas that were for the most part depopulated. Today, at their desired place of refuge, migrants encounter societies that are not necessarily geared to their arrival. The sheer scale of the global refugee crisis that we are now witnessing, along with its dynamism, poses a particular challenge for the community of nations.

Where are people fleeing from and to?

So, which regions and countries of the world are people fleeing from? At the end of 2015, the first and second places in this list were occupied by countries of the Near and Middle East which for years had been in the public eye as a result of the terror, conflict and forced expulsions being conducted there. By quite some margin, Syria was responsible for generating the greatest number of refugees; the country has been embroiled in a devastating civil war since 2011. By late 2015, some 4.9 million Syrians had been displaced. Of these, a million had made their way to Europe over the preceding 12 months alone. The large majority, though, were living along the country's borders, in huge refugee camps just inside Lebanon, Jordan and Turkey. In second place was Afghanistan, a country that has not been at peace since it was invaded by US and coalition troops in 2001 in the aftermath of the 9/11 attacks on New York and Washington. By the end of 2015, it was estimated to have produced around 2.7 million refugees.

These two countries have for years been at the centre of worldwide attention as a result of the conflicts and humanitarian crises taking place there. This is not true to anywhere near the same extent for the countries with the next-highest tallies of refugees. These are all African nations: Somalia (with 1.12 million refugees), South Sudan (779,000), Sudan (629,000) and the Democratic Republic of Congo (542,000). These, too, are countries whose civilian populations have been exposed to a succession of wars and other violent conflicts – even though these have attracted far less international attention. Somalia has been regarded for several years now as a failed state. The civil war of the 1990s was followed by a power vacuum. Bitter fighting ensued between enemy warlords and regional clans, and the failing structures of the states led to a rise of Islamist groupings, above all the terrorist militia known as Al-Shabaab (Arabic for 'the youth'), which now controls large parts of the country. In 2011, after many years of struggle, the largely Christian South Sudan finally gained its independence from the Muslim-dominated north of the country. All the hope that was associated with the formation of this new nation swiftly gave way to a tragic reality. Since 2013, a bloody civil war has raged in the newest country on Earth between different factions intent on gaining supremacy. The result has been thousands of dead and millions of displaced persons both within the country and outside it.

Within the list of the 10 countries responsible for creating the most refugees, alongside Myanmar and Colombia, there are two further African states: the Central African Republic – where the Muslim rebel movement Séléka seized power in a coup in 2013, resulting in 471,000 people fleeing their homes – and Eritrea, where an especially dictatorial regime has driven 411,000 people abroad.[7]

Many Europeans are convinced that their countries are shouldering the heaviest burden of the global refugee crisis, but, even though more than a million refugees made their way to Europe in 2015, the fact remains that some 86 per cent of refugees worldwide are in states outside Europe with low or average incomes. Many of these countries border on the conflict zones from which the people have fled in the first place. Globally, Turkey, with around 2.5 million refugees, is the largest of these host nations, followed by Pakistan (1.6 million refugees) and Lebanon (1.1 million). According to UNHCR statistics, of the

10 countries with the most refugees within their borders, no fewer than five were African: heading the list is Ethiopia, with 736,000 refugees, a large number of whom were from South Sudan and neighbouring Eritrea. This is followed by Kenya (554,000), Uganda (477,000), the Democratic Republic of Congo (383,000) and Chad (370,000).

These figures demonstrate that the main onus of the great mass migration movements taking place in Africa and the Middle East falls on the neighbouring states. In the case of Syria, these countries are (alongside Turkey) Lebanon, Jordan and Iraq. The picture is similar in Africa: the great majority of the almost 800,000 people who have fled South Sudan have found refuge in the surrounding countries – almost 300,000 in Ethiopia, 200,000 in Uganda, 195,000 in Sudan and 95,000 in Kenya. In turn, the refugees from the Central African Republic have been taken in primarily by the neighbouring states of Cameroon, the Democratic Republic of Congo, Chad and the Republic of Congo. The bulk of refugees thus find refuge in regions and countries with far worse economic and infrastructural frameworks than the industrialised nations of the West. At the end of 2015, almost 14 million refugees were living in so-called developing nations, as against just 2.2 million in industrialised nations.

Only since late 2015, when the mass migration of people to Europe really got under way, have the states of the EU started to face up, to a greater or lesser degree, to their responsibility within the worldwide refugee crisis. This becomes especially clear when one considers the number of refugees in relation to the total population of any given country: in 2015, Lebanon was at the top of this list with 183 refugees per 1,000 people in its population, followed by Jordan (87), the Pacific island state of Nauru (50), Turkey (32), Chad (26) and Djibouti (22).

A 'hard, stony place': Refugee camps in Africa

It is not just in the Near and Middle East that the number of refugees has risen massively in recent years: 4.4 million Africans were on the move at the end of 2015, 20 per cent more than in the preceding year. Most of these – some 2.74 million – came from East Africa and the Horn of Africa, while 1.2 million were fleeing from Central Africa and 190,000 from Southern Africa.[8]

The refugee camps that have been set up in the world's crisis regions continue to grow in size, with some of the largest being found in East Africa. Dadaab in Kenya, for example, is situated over 100 kilometres from the border with Somalia. It has been there for 25 years, having been erected in the desert region in 1992 to offer a place of refuge to Somalians fleeing the civil war in their country. The name 'Dadaab' translates into English as 'hard, stony place'. Over time, it grew into a chaotic city covering an area of 77 square kilometres – an endless sea of UN tents and temporary huts built of thornbush scrub, criss-crossed by dusty, unsurfaced roads. On occasion, there have been as many as 500,000 people living here, most of them Somalians. But Dadaab has also been home to Ethiopians escaping from the famine crisis in their country in 2011, along with refugees from Chad and Sudan. According to official UNHCR figures, the total number of people living there in April 2016 was 344,648, around 95 per cent of whom were Somalians.[9] Observers assume that the actual figure is considerably higher than this. Some 10,000 other people are camped outside the gates of the facility. They remain there, largely ignored by the world's press, in atrocious sanitary conditions without any hope or outlook for the future. The British journalist Ben Rawlence accompanied several inhabitants of the Dadaab refugee camp and wrote a moving book about their plight.[10] Many of the people there were born and have grown up at the camp – they have known no life outside its confines. The Kenyan administration forbids the refugees to work and rejects all measures that might help turn the temporary camp into a more permanent entity, such as asphalting the roads there. Feeding the inhabitants of Dadaab is the responsibility of the World Food Programme of the UN and various non-governmental organisations (NGOs), who also provide schooling and healthcare facilities. But the situation of the people living there has grown worse over the last few years, with UN food rations for Dadaab being cut several times in succession. The UN has simply been running out of money since aid for Syria was increased and member states slashed their contributions for African aid. The Kenyan government has repeatedly stated its intention to close down the camp – but how can a temporary city with half a million inhabitants simply vanish? Those living there cannot return to either Ethiopia or Somalia. So, what is to happen to all these people?

Two more vast African refugee camps are situated in Ethiopia: some 220,000 refugees principally from the neighbouring country of South Sudan are living in a camp at Gambela in the west of the country, while at Dollo Ado in the east around 210,000 from Somalia have found shelter. Tanzania and Uganda have also for a long time been providing aid for refugees on a large scale. For instance, the Adjumani camp in northern Uganda is home primarily to refugees from South Sudan; as of autumn 2015, the camp housed over 110,000 people. Meanwhile, in the east of Tanzania, about 150 kilometres from Lake Tanganyika, stands the Nyarugusu camp. This facility was built by the UN in 1996, at a time when more than 100,000 people were fleeing from a bloody civil war in the Democratic Republic of Congo, crossing Lake Tanganyika in boats to get to Tanzania. More recently, the camp has seen an influx of refugees from Burundi, escaping from unrest in their home country. Today, there are some 152,000 people living in Nyarugusu. Here, too, one can see serried ranks of white-grey tents bearing the light blue UN logo, stretching seemingly endlessly into the distance, between muddy reddish-brown tracks bordered by home-made clay ovens where people cook their food. 'In your whole life, pray to God never to be called a "refugee", even for a single day,' declares Euphrasie Munyerenkana, who fled from the Congo to Nyarugusu as a *mkimbizi* (the Swahili term for a refugee) and who has been living in the camp for many years:

> To be called a refugee is such an uncomfortable status that there is nothing to compare to it. First, a refugee is a person in someone else's hand. You have no hands or legs anymore, you are fed and clothed. You have your eyes, but you can't see anything. You have a mouth to speak but you can't say anything. You have ears to listen but you can't hear anything. You have a nose to smell but you can't smell anything. Basically, you are abandoned to your fate. God granted us life, only He knows our whereabouts. We are in no condition to live like human beings.[11]

While the world has focused its concern on Syria, it has scarcely paid any attention to the exodus of millions of people from East Africa. When Ben Rawlence travelled to Washington at the invitation of the US National Security Council, in order to brief the members of this body on conditions in the camp at Dadaab, he found that his audience was interested in only one subject: did the camp represent a source of threat to US security and was there any danger of its inhabitants becoming radicalised and joining the Islamist Al-Shabaab organisation? Yet the people in that camp had fled precisely from such extremists. The US, it seemed, was not interested in the humanitarian plight of the millions of refugees in Africa's camps; nor were the other industrialised states of the West. The key thing in their eyes was that the refugees did not become Islamist terrorists who could pose a threat to the West.[12]

The 'Arc of Instability'

The American administration talks in terms of an 'Arc of Instability' stretching from Mali in the west of Africa through Nigeria, Chad and Sudan and then further across the Red Sea in the direction of Yemen, Saudi Arabia, Pakistan and Afghanistan. Even this assessment has been conducted largely from the viewpoint of growing extremism and the so-called War on Terror, which characterised American policy on Africa, as in other areas, following the attacks of 9/11. The terrorist network Al-Qaeda first launched its campaign against the US from African soil, three years before the airliner attacks took place on the World Trade Center and the Pentagon. On 7 August 1998, two car bombs exploded almost simultaneously outside the US embassies in the capitals of Kenya and Tanzania. The first bomb, which had been planted on a small truck, caused the façade of the embassy building in Nairobi to collapse; 201 Kenyans and 12 Americans were killed. Most of the Kenyan victims were passers-by, along with the passengers on a commuter bus that happened to be driving past at the time of the explosion. Outside the US embassy in Dar-es-Salaam, several hundred kilometres to the south, a second bomb exploded very shortly afterwards, claiming the lives of 11 more people. The number of wounded in both attacks ran into the thousands. The leader of Al-Qaeda, Osama bin Laden, had previously lived in Sudan for five years and directed his operations from a base there.

In Mali, an offshoot of the Al-Qaeda terror organisation styling itself 'Al-Qaeda in the Islamic Maghreb' (AQIM) arose, occasionally joining forces with Tuareg rebels in the region. The Tuareg live a nomadic life on the fringes of the Sahara desert and have long been fighting there for a separate state. Together, these forces succeeded, in 2012, in defeating the Malian army and conquering the whole of the north of the country, including the city of Timbuktu. Ultimately, the Islamists turned on their former allies the Tuareg and began to introduce sharia law in territory governed by the nomads. The de facto establishment of an Al-Qaeda state in the Sahara prompted the West to intervene: with the support of the UN, Operation Serval was launched in January 2013, led by the French, the former colonial power in Mali. Within a few months, French and Malian forces managed to liberate the most important towns of the region from the control of AQIM.

The conflicts in Mali unleashed a large wave of refugees. The UNHCR estimated that around 150,000 refugees from Mali had fled to neighbouring countries, in addition to identifying 230,000 displaced persons within the country itself. On 1 March 2015, a peace treaty was concluded between armed groups from the north and the Malian government, yet the conflict was anything but resolved. Since then, there have been a number of attacks on the capital, Bamako, and other locations. In November 2015, Islamist terrorists assaulted the Hotel Radisson Blu in Bamako and killed 20 people. A few days later, a camp of UN peacekeeping troops in Kidal was bombarded with rockets. Clearly, the military intervention by France and the UN has not succeeded in pacifying the country. All that has happened is that the battlefield has shifted: the threat has moved from the Sahara to the densely populated south. There, the Islamists are currently on the advance, especially the group

calling itself the 'Front de libération du Massina', which oper-
ates across borders and whose aim is the establishment of a new
caliphate in the region.

In Nigeria, meanwhile, the group Boko Haram has been
making headlines. The organisation has launched especially
brutal attacks against both Christian targets and Muslims
who do not support it. Its Hausa name is an expression of its
agenda – one possible translation of it is 'books are a sin', while
another is 'Western education is a disgrace'. Its members dream
of the return of an age before democracy, education and the
rule of law existed. In just a few years, Boko Haram has developed from a small, obscure sect into a terror organisation that
can muster around 5,000 rebels. They have rampaged across
northern Nigeria with an almost nihilistic destructive reign of
terror, attacking Christian churches during Mass and mosques
during Friday prayers, bombing police stations and public
institutions, attacking mobile phone masts, storming schools
and laying waste to entire towns and villages. In May 2013,
in light of the ongoing attacks, Nigeria's president Goodluck
Jonathan announced the imposition of a state of emergency
in the federal states of Borno, Yobe and Adamawa. By that
time, more than 4,000 people had been killed by the terrorist
group.[13] Many women were kidnapped, raped and forced into
marriage. In April 2014, Boko Haram gained special notoriety
worldwide when they attacked the town of Chibok in the state
of Borno and abducted 219 schoolgirls. According to figures
from the UN children's organisation, UNICEF, repeated
attacks by Boko Haram in both Nigeria and the adjoining
states of Cameroon, Niger and Chad have led to the closure of
more than 2,000 schools. For their part, the Nigerian army has
conducted its anti-insurgency campaign against Boko Haram
with the utmost brutality, thus causing the civilian populace

even greater hardship. Many people fear the army as much as they do the terrorists of Boko Haram. According to Amnesty International, there were more than 2.1 million internal refugees in northern Nigeria in late 2015. Of these, more than a million were children and young people.[14] These young refugees have been housed in a camp in Maiduguri, where there is a serious lack of sanitation and food, or have been dispersed throughout many villages and hamlets across the country.

In Somalia, the aforementioned Islamist militia Al-Shabaab controls large areas of the south of the country, where it has rigidly imposed sharia law. It has made the creation of an Islamic state on the Horn of Africa its primary objective and regards itself as part of a worldwide jihad. In recent years, the organisation has tried to draw attention to its cause by conducting terror attacks beyond the borders of Somalia. For example, it claimed responsibility for an attack on the Ugandan capital Kampala on 11 July 2010, when bombs were set off in two bars during the screening of the football World Cup Final, killing 74 people. Al-Shabaab also claimed responsibility for the attack on the Westgate Shopping Mall in the Kenyan capital of Nairobi on 21 September 2013 – an atrocity that claimed the lives of 67 people, with hundreds more wounded. The terror campaign of Al-Shabaab has also triggered a great wave of refugees. Hundreds of thousands of Somalians are now living not only in Dadaab but also in many other refugee camps in neighbouring states.

This overview of the activities of Boko Haram, AQIM and Al-Shabaab only captures a tiny fraction of the reality of modern Africa. It is not only the fear of terror and displacement that drives people in Africa to flee their homes. The reasons why so many people in Africa do not see a future for themselves on their continent any longer are more numerous and varied than the categories at our disposal here. The definitions of political and religious persecution, of enforced flight on one hand and voluntary migration on the other, are inadequate tools for really grasping the circumstances of people's lives. The fates of human beings are not susceptible to being neatly pigeonholed. Anyone who fears for his life because he doesn't have enough to eat finds himself in just as desperate a situation as a person who is being persecuted for his faith or his political convictions. Food and water shortages, a lack of work, an inadequate educational system and a non-existent health service: can a person escaping such a situation be said to be fleeing voluntarily? As the Nigerian-American author Teju Cole has written: 'Sometimes the gun aimed at your head is grinding poverty, or endless shabby struggle...'[15]

'Good' and 'bad' refugees

The notional distinction between (enforced) flight and (voluntary) migration, between 'good' refugees, namely those who are being persecuted politically, and the 'bad' ones – the so-called economic migrants – does not do the real situation on the ground justice. One may well assuage one's conscience in thereby reducing the historical dimensions of migration to a scale that is humanly graspable. We grant one group, namely refugees, the right to seek out another place for themselves on Earth, while denying it to the other group, namely migrants. Yet this kind of categorisation also obscures our view of the extent and the reasons for the worldwide movement of refugees that we find ourselves confronted by, and especially the exodus from Africa. Poverty, hunger, wars and crises have driven people to make the momentous decision to leave their homeland. But above all it is a general lack of prospects that is driving Africans from their homes. Most people who have attended high school have no hope of ever finding work in their country of origin. In Ethiopia in 2012, for example, there were some 35,000 graduates who had completed their course of studies with a bachelor's degree, yet only 5 per cent of them could find paid employment in their home country. Anyone who takes a room at the Sheraton Hotel in Addis Ababa can be certain that the chambermaid who serves coffee there has a bachelor's degree to her name. It is not the poorest of the poor who undertake the arduous journey to Europe. The poorest of the poor do not even have the wherewithal to flee. Desperation may drive them from one place to the next, but they do not have the means necessary to organise their flight from the country or to pay traffickers. It is Africa's future that is leaving the continent.

Most refugees who set out for Europe come from the lower middle classes. Money is collected within their families so that they can embark on the dangerous journey. For the person's relatives it is an investment in the future. One of their number who is healthy and robust is being sent on his way. If he makes it to Europe, they speculate, he will send most of what he earns there back home – and in this way he will be able to feed them all.

Yet the urge for a better life is also omnipresent among those who have nothing. In Dadaab and other Kenyan camps, for example, the Somali word *buufis* has become common currency, particularly among young people: it means 'a desire to relocate'. Most of the older people in the refugee camps would like more than anything to go back to their homes immediately, but the situation is different among the young. It is their objective to make it through to the Maghreb states and from there to get to Europe, the US or Australia. Their feet may still be firmly rooted in the camp, but their heads are already far away from Africa.[16] They yearn to find a safe place where they can build a life for themselves. Who can begrudge them this wish?

Escape routes

For the vast majority of refugees, there is no legal way of fulfilling their dream of Europe. In consequence, they are forced to rely upon traffickers and smugglers. In the midst of poverty, people-smuggling has become a stable source of income, and latterly an even more lucrative trade than the smuggling of arms and drugs. Most Africans who set off on the dangerous trek try initially to make it to the Maghreb states, namely to Morocco, Tunisia, Algeria or Libya. The journey undertaken by people from west Africa – from Gambia, Côte d'Ivoire, Nigeria and other states – leads via the Western Mediterranean route to ports in Algeria and Morocco. From there it is just a few kilometres across the sea to Spain. The West African or Central Mediterranean route leads through Niger to Libya. There refugees embark on boats bound for the Italian islands of Lampedusa or Sicily. In its turn, the Eastern Mediterranean route leads via Turkey, from the harbours of Izmir or Bodrum to Greek offshore islands in the Aegean such as Lesbos. Many people have also reached Europe via the overland route through Turkey; starting out from Istanbul, they have made it through to the Greek or Bulgarian borders. In the process they have to cross the River Evros, which can easily be forded in summer, or find their way across the wooded border into Bulgaria.

In 2014, the European frontier protection agency Frontex registered 283,000 so-called irregular migrants at the external borders of Europe. By 2015, that number had already increased more than sixfold to a total of 1,820,400.[17] Syrians and Afghans (594,000 and 267,500 irregular migrants, respectively) represented the largest groups among this number. In 2015, most people fled via the Eastern Mediterranean route from Turkey to the Greek islands. Frontex recorded around 154,000 'irregular' border crossings on the Central Mediterranean route, with Italy as the destination; on this route, the predominant group of refugees was Eritreans (38,800), followed by Nigerians (22,000) and Somalis (12,500). On the Western Mediterranean route, with the end destination of Spain, some 7,200 people made it to Europe by irregular means. These included almost 2,000 people from Guinea, 1,052 from Algeria and 828 from Morocco.[18] In terms of percentage, people from Africa did not represent the majority of frontier crossings registered by Frontex; the preeminent nationalities were Syrians (33 per cent), Afghans (15 per cent) and Iraqis (6 per cent). Far behind these came people from Eritrea (2 per cent), and Nigeria, Somalia and Morocco (each 1 per cent).[19] The fact of the matter is this: the civil war in Syria will eventually come to an end, whereas the situation in Africa will not change for the better at any time soon. Meanwhile, an increasing number of people are toying with the idea of leaving their homeland. Africa is sitting with its bags packed.

'Mare Monstrum'

Since March 2016, when the EU signed a refugee agreement with Turkey that effectively closed off the so-called Balkan route, the numbers of people trying to cross the Mediterranean to Greece have fallen off dramatically. According to figures issued by the UNHCR, around 150,000 refugees landed on Greek soil from January to May 2016.[20] By contrast, the numbers of those trying to reach Italy by boat have risen sharply once more. From January to the beginning of June 2016, around 50,000 refugees arrived in Italy – predominantly Africans. Around half of them hailed from Nigeria, Gambia, Somalia, Eritrea and Côte d'Ivoire. They belong to the group of people who have survived the perilous crossing of the Mediterranean; for many others, the dream of Europe has ended in death. From 2014 to the beginning of June 2016, the UNHCR estimated that some 10,000 refugees were drowned in the Mediterranean. From its traditional designation as 'Mare Nostrum', it has become a 'Mare Monstrum'. The probability of losing one's life making the dangerous crossing from Africa to Italy is 1 in 23.[21]

No one knows precisely how many people have died while attempting to flee their homeland and make a new life elsewhere. Nobody keeps a count of the numbers of those who die while trying to cross the Sahara. There are no television pictures available from the desert. But to judge from the accounts of those who have successfully made this journey, we know how deadly dangerous this passage can be. The crossing on small pickup trucks, organised by smugglers, generally takes three days. Dozens of people sit hunched together on the flatbeds of these vehicles. So as not to lose their grip during the journey, they jam sticks into the flatbed and cling tightly to them. Anyone who falls from the vehicle is abandoned to their fate. A person's life counts for very little in the eyes of the smugglers. Women report sexual assaults and rapes. Bandits attack the vehicles, and, in the case of a breakdown, the journey has to be completed on foot. The International Organization for Migration works on the assumption that more people die on the route across the Sahara than those who perish in the Mediterranean. In the first six months of 2016 alone, the organisation counted 3,694 people who had died while making their way to a new homeland, most of them en route to Europe.[22]

The Italian newspaper *Il Giornale* wrote in May 2016 that Europe would have to reckon with an influx of more than half a million refugees from Kenya alone. People were said to be attempting to get from East Africa to Libya and from there to embark on boats across the Mediterranean, with the aim of making it to Italy. The talk was of an exodus of Biblical proportions.[23] The background to this story was the announcement shortly prior to this by the Kenyan government that Dadaab and another large refugee camp on Kenyan soil were to be closed. The Kenyan interior cabinet secretary Joseph Nkaissery maintained that this policy would be implemented by the end of 2016. In addition, observers and human rights organisations are reckoning with an increasing number of refugees from the Central African Republic, Mali, the Democratic Republic of Congo, Gambia and other countries. No one can predict exactly how many people will join the exodus, but there is no doubt that the number of Africans who are entertaining this possibility is huge.

Tens of thousands of Africans who have made it to Libya across the Sahara are now languishing there, waiting for the opportunity to cross to Europe. Many of them have been arrested and detained as illegal migrants in overcrowded reception camps in towns like Misrata.[24] Nobody in this tumbledown city looks after their welfare, least of all the embassies of the countries from which they have fled. On the beaches of the west coast, from where the traffickers' boats leave for Europe, the refugees can see the washed-up, bloated corpses of those who did not survive the crossing. The sight does not deter them from taking the risk themselves. You feel like shouting out to them: 'Listen! Don't you know that people in Europe have economic problems, too? You must realise that Europe can't take all the refugees who want to come there! Do you have any idea what's in store for you there? You'll be put in a reception camp along with thousands of other refugees. You'll have to wait for ages before even being allowed to file an application for asylum. And, during that time, you won't be allowed to work.' But the young Africans know all that. They don't live in the back of beyond. They have smartphones and internet access. They have friends and relatives who have already made it to Europe and who tell them what life there is like.

They are, no doubt, also well aware that not all people in Europe are well disposed towards them, and that there have been several attacks on refugee hostels. Europeans should be under no illusions: in comparison to the life that refugees have been forced to lead in their countries of origin, life as an asylum seeker in Germany, the UK, Sweden or elsewhere looks positively like paradise. I do not know of any African who has left his family, his friends and his familiar environment just because he thinks he can earn more elsewhere than in his home country. They leave their homelands because they cannot survive there or because, for fear of persecution, they are not in a position to breathe freely. They leave everything behind, pack together the bare essentials and embark on their journeys with heavy hearts – and no risk appears too great to them on their odysseys.

One needs to face up to this reality in order to finally begin to tackle the problem and to combat its deep-seated causes: we must improve the living conditions of people in Africa so that this exodus does not come about in the first place. Only when people identify a future within their own homelands will they stay put. Europe should not succumb to the fantasy that this mass migration can somehow be stemmed by sea patrols, or by putting up fences and walls.

In the eighteenth century, people in Europe wrested the right to freedom and the principle of basic human dignity from their autocratic rulers. 'All human beings are born free and equal in dignity and rights' – thus runs Article 1 of the Universal Declaration of Human Rights adopted by the UN in December 1948. We should constantly bear in mind that this principle applies to every person, in Europe as well as Africa and other parts of the world, irrespective of the colour of their skin, or whether they are poor, rich, firmly ensconced in their homeland or a refugee in a foreign place.

2

THE LEGACY OF COLONIALISM

'Internally, Africa and Europe are as unlike one another as an elephant and an ant,' wrote the Somalia-born novelist Nuruddin Farah.[25] With its surface area of 30.3 million square kilometres, Africa is the second-largest continent on Earth after Asia. It is twice as big as India and China put together, and you could fit 10 Europes into it. Today, Africa is home to some 16 per cent of the world's population – around 1.2 billion people. A hundred years ago, that figure was only around 120 to 130 million. In the 54 states that comprise modern Africa there are literally thousands of different ethnicities, 2,000 distinct languages, the most diverse cultures and a host of different religions. By contrast, Europe is the second-smallest continent. With around 740 million inhabitants, it currently makes up some 10 per cent of the global population yet only contains just over 60 languages. Of course, all this is just a snapshot, for, according to population experts, it will not be long before the ratio looks quite different: by the year 2100, it is estimated that Europe's population will have shrunk to 650 million, while Africa's will have almost quadrupled to 4.4 billion. Based on those figures, only about 6 per cent of people on Earth will be living in Europe, while Africa will be home to fully 39 per cent.[26]

The history of relations between Africa and Europe is a long one. For 2,000 years, Africa was a 'continent of adventure' for Europe. Its inhabitants were either 'primitives', 'cannibals' or 'noble savages'. The writer Rudyard Kipling saw Europeans as a parade of marching army boots trampling across Africa: 'We're foot—slog—slog—slog—sloggin' over Africa / Foot—foot—foot—foot—sloggin' over Africa— / (Boots—boots—boots—boots—movin' up and down again!)'[27] Furthermore, it was Europe that was largely responsible for the fact that, for centuries, the vast area of the world that was Africa had such a relatively small population. The European colonialists infected Africans with new diseases against which they had no opportunity to develop immunity, such as smallpox, measles and cholera. In the centuries of the transatlantic slave trade, from the fifteenth to the nineteenth century, Arab and European slave traders put millions of Africans in shackles and forced them to leave their home continent.

Africa even owes its name to Europeans. In 146 BC, the Romans conquered the city of Carthage, which was situated close to the modern city of Tunis, and soon after they founded the province of Africa. The Romans called its inhabitants 'Afra', after the indigenous people whom they encountered there; according to modern scholars, the Afri were a Berber tribe living along the banks of the River Bagrada in present-day Tunisia. Over the course of time, the Romans applied the name of the province Africa first to North Africa and ultimately to the entire continent. Yet, while the Europeans, making no attempt at differentiation, saw the continent as a single entity, this was by no means the perception of its native peoples. Over the centuries they identified themselves primarily through their communities based on family, clan, ethnicity and language.

Europe's 'Dark Continent'

For a long time, the Europeans knew very little about the African continent and indeed showed very little interest in it – which, apart from anything else, undoubtedly had to do with its sheer size. For one thing, in classical antiquity and the Middle Ages, Europeans were familiar with only a very small part of Africa. For the Romans, Aethiopia, or the land of the 'burned faces', ended at the Second Cataract of the Nile. On the other hand, for Europeans of the medieval period, Cape Bojador on the northwest coast marked the end of the world. The Portuguese were the first Europeans to land on the west coast of Africa. In 1487, Bartolomeu Dias 'discovered' the southern tip of Africa and gave it the name 'Cape of the Storms'. Around the turn of the century 10 years later, in 1497–98, Vasco da Gama rounded the same headland and rechristened it the 'Cape of Good Hope'. He went on to sail up the east coast of Africa as far as Kenya; his aim was to try and find a southerly sea route to India.

Another 150 years would elapse before the Dutch became the first European nation to establish a permanent settlement in Africa. In 1652, a supply station was built at the Cape of Good Hope for ships of the Dutch East India Company (Vereenigde Oostindische Compagnie) to take on board provisions for their onward journeys. Penetration into the continent's interior was a slow and arduous affair. The vegetation seemed impenetrable and full of insects that were vectors of unknown diseases. For Europeans, Africa was the 'Dark Continent', a phrase in which the epithet 'dark' referred both to the aspect of the unknown and to the skin colour of those who lived there. And yet, as is well known, many Africans, then as now, are not dark-skinned, with many North and also South Africans having a light skin tone. Also, the ancestors of 'white' Europeans were ultimately

dark-skinned. The European population only began to 'turn
pale' around 6,000 years ago.

All European nations that ventured into Africa shared the
firm conviction that they were bringing civilisation with them.
They could and would not entertain the notion that Africa had
already been home to some highly advanced civilisations. In
the Middle Ages in Europe, a legend began to circulate that
a large and powerful Christian empire existed somewhere in
Africa, ruled by a figure called Prester John. It was rumoured
that, in around 1160, this mythical priest-king – the 'King of
Kings at the ends of the Earth' – had sent a letter to the ruler
of Byzantium in which he described the manifold virtues of
his realm. He asserted that no fewer than 72 kings were his
vassals, and that he commanded a huge army. His palace displayed a unique splendour: the walls and floors were made of
onyx, he claimed, and the dining tables of gold and amethyst.
His bedchamber was decked out with wonderful decorations
in gold and encrusted with precious stones, while the bed itself
was made entirely of sapphire. The famous world map drawn
up by the Spanish seafarer Juan de la Cosa in 1500 shows the
supposed empire of Prester John located north of Ethiopia and
west of the Nile.

African empires

European rulers hoped that the mythical priest-king in the
dark heart of Africa might lend them his support in their cru-
sades against the rising force of Islam. The fact that a great
Christian empire really did exist in Ethiopia at that time went
beyond their powers of comprehension. As early as AD 350,
King Ezana proclaimed Christianity to be the official religion
of his Kingdom of Axum. This polity, which encompassed

parts of present-day Ethiopia, Eritrea, Sudan and Yemen, survived until the beginning of the ninth century. The spread of Islam eventually led to its downfall. There were highly developed societies and kingdoms in other parts of Africa, too, which had been in existence for several centuries and which were fully on a par with comparable European institutions of the same period. The Empire of Mali, for example, which ruled over large parts of West Africa from the thirteenth to the seventeenth century, was the second-largest empire in the world at that time, exceeded only by the Mongol Empire. The federally structured Kingdom of Wolof, meanwhile, which covered the territory of modern Senegal and the Gambia, endured for over half a millennium before finally losing its independence in 1890 and becoming subsumed within the colonial federation of 'French West Africa'. The West African Ashanti Empire held sway for over 200 years, from 1680 to 1896, before being overrun by the British. At the height of its power, it embraced the whole area covered by the modern Republic of Ghana.

From the sixteenth to the nineteenth century, the territory of the present-day Democratic Republic of Congo comprised the Kingdom of Luba. Power was shared by the king (who was known by the designation 'Mulopwe') and a council of noblemen called the Bamfumus. Art was held in high esteem in Luba, as evidenced by the famous wooden statues attributed to an artist known as the Master of Buli. In December 2010, Sotheby's in Paris sold one of these works for €5.4 million ($7.1 million).[28] Such impressive testaments to advanced civilisations can be found throughout Africa: for instance, Egypt's ancient pyramids at Memphis and Nubian rock temples at Abu Simbel, both of which are thousands of years old; the stelae at Axum (third to fourth centuries AD), which is on the same site as the Church of Our Lady Mary of Zion, the oldest church in Ethiopia (and where, according to the ancient traditions of the Ethiopian Orthodox Church, the Ark of the Covenant is kept); the stone circles at Wassu in the Gambia, which date from the eighth century; the monolithic stone churches at Lalibela in Ethiopia, which were hewn directly out of the rock of a hillside in around 1250; the adobe mosques of Timbuktu from the fourteenth and fifteenth centuries; the Royal Palaces of Abomey in Benin; and many others. Important rock paintings, which in some cases date back up to 2,500 years, can be found in such places as Tassili n'Ajjer in Algeria, Tadrart Acacus in Libya, the Tsodilo Hills in Botswana and Chongoni in Malawi. All these are now on the list of UNESCO World Heritage Sites.

To all of this – African civilisations, their societies, their cultural achievements and their languages – the European colonialists were blind. They regarded the Africans as 'naked savages' and 'barbarians', who had remained at mankind's primitive stage and were devoid of their own culture and history. The settlers also lacked any understanding of the Africans' community-orientated thinking, a concept commonly encapsulated nowadays in a term deriving from the Xhosa and Zulu languages of South Africa: ubuntu. People saw (and still see) themselves as constituent parts of a whole. There were no hard-and-fast boundaries between the kingdoms, villages and communities, as there were in Europe. Allegiances were to families, clans, tribal leaders and councils of elders, but not to a state. And, unlike in Europe, private property was virtually unknown; whatever one possessed was shared as common property. The philosophy of ubuntu continues to characterise large parts of Africa to this day – and it is the source of countless misunderstandings and difficulties in dealings between Europeans and Africans.

The trauma of slavery

On the heels of the Portuguese colonists came the French, Dutch, English, Belgians and Scandinavians, as well as the German and Ottoman empires. They were driven by a lust to acquire gold, ivory and slaves. In other parts of the world, such as the Americas and Asia, indigenous populations suffered the ruthless depredations of European conquerors, but nowhere were the effects as disastrous as in Africa. Certainly, slavery had existed before the arrival of Europeans, but it had been conducted on a scale that had no comparison with the transatlantic slave trade instituted by the conquerors. Slaves were traditionally regarded in the main as family members; not infrequently they also had the opportunity to purchase their freedom. The Europeans, however, put in place a system of human trafficking. To them, people in Africa were nothing more than heads of livestock or commodities that they could sell at a profit. Families were torn apart; millions of men, women and children were taken captive and forcibly transported to other parts of the world. Many of them ended up in Europe – in 1500, for instance, black slaves made up one-tenth of the population of Lisbon. Later, most slaves were transported to North or South America. In 1760, the British colony of Virginia contained 200,000 black slaves; across the 13 American colonies belonging to Great Britain, black slaves accounted for 30 per cent of the population. On the massive plantations growing cotton, tobacco and sugar cane, they were employed as a workforce without any rights whatsoever. On these large-scale enterprises, the demand for slave labour became positively insatiable, after the indigenous population of the Americas had been decimated by wars and epidemics of imported diseases.

Initially, Portugal enjoyed a monopoly on the African slave trade. The Portuguese were supplanted in time by the

Spanish, who ran the traffic in human beings as a state monopoly until the eighteenth century, then sold on their rights to other nations and private traders. In doing so, they relied on a network of Arab and African manhunters who captured their quarry in the interior and then sold them on to the Europeans at the coast. One document attesting to the inhumanity of the slave trade comes from the year 1696. In it, the Portuguese Guinea Company is granted permission to import annually '10,000 tonnes of negroes'.[29]

Estimates of how many Africans in total were deported from their homeland vary wildly – some scholars work on the basis of up to 50 million people, but in any event we may state with certainty that the figure was over 12 million.[30] Furthermore, no one can say how many died while being hunted down, during the passage to the American colonies and while engaged in slave labour itself. The crime of the abduction of millions of people in Africa by Europeans still weighs heavily on the continent to this day. Yet it also remains an incontrovertible fact that the whole vast scale of the slave trade would not have been possible without the complicity not only of African and Arab slave traders but also of local tribal chiefs who profited from handing over their neighbours.

Europe's 'Scramble for Africa'

The forerunners of European colonists in Africa were explorers, adventurers, missionaries and merchants. In 1795, the Scotsman Mungo Park was one of the first European explorers to journey into the interior of the continent. He was followed by the German Heinrich Barth and the Scottish missionary David Livingstone, both of whom explored large tracts of the African interior in the nineteenth century. Other explorers included Richard Burton, John Speke and James Grant, who ventured to the great lakes of East Africa and went in search of the sources of the Nile. By the mid-nineteenth century around 10 per cent of Africa was under European control. The most important colonies were Angola, which was governed by Portugal; the British Cape Colony; and Algeria, to which France laid claim. Ivory, natural rubber, tea and coffee were all sought-after 'colonial goods' in the domestic markets of European countries.

Progressive industrialisation, the development of steam navigation and the railways, the telegraph and advances in medicine all drove European expansion in Africa. Before long, Africa became a bone of contention for rival European imperial states, prompting the start of the 'Scramble for Africa'. France occupied Tunisia and the area of the present-day Republic of Congo in 1881, followed by Guinea in 1884. Great Britain claimed the Ottoman protectorate of Egypt for itself in 1882, while Italy took possession of parts of Eritrea. The German Second Empire, in its turn, seized the coastal regions of Togo and Cameroon as well as – under the command of the Bremen tobacco merchant Adolf Lüderitz – an area initially known as 'Lüderitzland', a coastal strip from which the colony of 'German South West Africa' (modern Namibia) later developed. The young kingdom of Belgium – which had only come into being in 1830 – also wanted a slice of 'ce magnifique gâteau africain'.[31] In 1876, the Belgian king Leopold II proclaimed the formation of the 'Congo Free State'.

In November 1884, the German Imperial Chancellor Otto von Bismarck invited 13 European states and the Ottoman Empire to a conference in Berlin. The conference room in the Chancellor's palace on the Wilhelmstraße was dominated by a huge, five-metre-high map of Africa. At this highly dubious

gathering, which went down in history as the 'Congo Conference', the European powers divided up the African continent,
with its more than 150 separate peoples, between themselves.
The sovereignty rights of Africans over their own territories
were simply swept aside. Their land, which in the view of the
colonial powers was just 'virgin territory' (*terra nullius*), was
declared 'crown property', which could be disposed of at will
to colonial trading companies, concessionaries and settlers.
The whole enterprise was dressed up in a cloak of high-minded
aspiration: the Europeans had a 'civilising mission' to conduct
in Africa, and a duty to improve the 'moral and material welfare
of its indigenous peoples.'[32] The European nations assembled
in Berlin drew lines on the map using a ruler to demarcate
their claimed spheres of interest – ignoring in the process
geographical factors and the ethnic composition of the populations living there. The countries that were signatories to the
ensuing General Act of the Berlin Conference determined that
any power that actually took possession of a region should have
the right to establish a colony there ('effective occupation').
The Belgian king managed to gain his European colleagues'
consent to the proposal that the Congo – which, with its more
than 2 million square kilometres, covered an area the size of the
whole of Western Europe – should be transferred to his private
possession.

Not a single African representative attended this conference – Africans were the object rather than the subject of this
smash-and-grab seizure of an entire continent, the likes of
which had not been witnessed before, nor have been replicated
since. Africa was seen as a self-evident possession of Europe –
and quite unashamedly the European countries proceeded to
divide the spoils amongst themselves. Even Ethiopia, the only
state in Africa at that time to have retained its independence,

was not invited to Berlin. Its territory was assigned to the Kingdom of Italy's 'sphere of influence'. Yet the sense of astonishment in Europe was great when, not long afterwards, Italy's attempt to invade the African continent and take possession of Ethiopia met with a resounding military defeat. In the Battle of Adowa on 1 March 1896, Ethiopian troops – barefoot and armed for the most part with spears and shields – emerged victorious against an Italian force that was superior in both military technology and numbers.

Thus it was that Ethiopia – together with Liberia, where, from the 1820s onwards, the USA had begun sending its freed slaves – remained the only African country that was able to avoid the clutches of the European colonial powers. Large parts of the Sahara became French. Great Britain harboured a dream of a colonial empire that would stretch from Egypt to South Africa ('from the Cape to Cairo'). In 1899 it picked a fight with the Orange Free State and Transvaal Boer republics, lured by the potential profits to be gleaned from the gold and diamond deposits there. The Second Boer War ended in 1902 with the incorporation of the Boer states into the British Empire. In 1911, France and Spain divided Morocco between themselves. In 1914, the Sultanate of Egypt, which had been under British control since 1882, was formally annexed and declared a British protectorate – this was the final building block in the occupation of Africa by Europe on the eve of the First World War.

'Hottentots' and Herero: German South West Africa

How could it happen that such a vast continent with around 120 million inhabitants and well-developed structures was subjugated within such a short space of time by a comparatively small number of foreign conquerors? This came about not least because the Europeans had the benefit of two inventions: large-scale production of the medication quinine as a preventative measure against malaria, and the development of the machine gun, against which native peoples had no defence. Resistance on their part was put down with extreme brutality. A tragic example of this was the way in which the Germans dealt with the Herero in German South West Africa. At the Congo Conference in Berlin, this region had been declared a protectorate of the German Empire; eight years later, in 1892, it was annexed by German settlers. The Nama people – whom the Germans called 'Hottentots' – and the Herero, both of whom had inhabited the region for centuries, were first deprived of their livelihoods by the new colonial masters. They were driven from their pasturages and their herds of cattle were confiscated. Instead, they were forced to hire themselves out as cheap labour on farms or in factories run by Germans. When the Herero eventually rose up against their oppressors, overrunning German farms and killing around 100 settlers, a force of around 15,000 German troops under the command of Lieutenant-General Lothar von Trotha was dispatched to German South West Africa. In a proclamation to the Herero issued on 2 October 1904, von Trotha ordered them to leave the country immediately and stated: 'If the Herero refuse to comply, I will make them do so by force of arms.' The proclamation continued: 'Any Herero found within the borders of the German territory, with or without a weapon and with or without cattle, will be summarily shot. I refuse to take in any more women and children; I will order them to be either driven back to their people or to be fired upon.'[33]

Lieutenant-General von Trotha's infamous 'order to shoot' aimed at the total annihilation of the Herero. Two months prior to the decree, the German troops had engaged in battle with the Herero at Waterberg. Even today historians are still divided over whether the German protection force intentionally drove the rebels into the Omaheke Desert or whether the Herero withdrew there of their own accord. What is beyond dispute, though, is that thousands upon thousands of them died of hunger, thirst and exhaustion in this inhospitable terrain. In addition, tens of thousands of Herero and Nama were either massacred by the German force or deported to concentration camps, where many perished from diseases or malnutrition. By 1911, of the original Herero population numbering around 80,000 to 100,000 people, only some 15,000 survived. That meant that 65,000 to 85,000 Herero, along with 10,000 Nama, had been slaughtered. The massacre of the Herero has gone down in history as the twentieth century's first act of genocide.[34]

Pseudo-scientific social Darwinist theories of the superiority of the 'Aryan race' legitimised the ruthless conduct of the German colonists. Time and again, Africans were treated to the same sermon: you are uneducated, uncivilised and worthless. 'We must never let the Negro win,' an outraged German citizen wrote to Kaiser Wilhelm II in 1904 apropos of the Herero revolt. He went on: 'What would become of the world after such a victory? Even now, the Negroes imagine Africa belongs to them rather than to our Lord God.'[35] Not only in Germany's colonies was the 'hippo whip', made from the hides of hippos or rhinos, used on a daily basis to punish the African populace. In 1907 the German colonial minister Bernhard Dernburg submitted the following report on conditions in German East Africa:

In Dar-es-Salaam almost all the white men went walking carrying a whip [...] I found one on the cash desk at the main bank, and in the station office or on the Usumbara railway, they were lying ready right next to the inkwell, and almost every white man took the opportunity to start thrashing any random Black who took his fancy.[36]

Direct and indirect rule

The various colonial regimes left their mark on Africa. They changed the entire political, economic and social fabric of the continent. This was not just a result of the borders that the colonial masters had so arbitrarily drawn. Traditional political and administrative structures were done away with, and intact communities and economic systems destroyed. In the General Act concluded at the end of the Berlin Congress, the signatories announced the abolition of slavery in Africa. Yet in many colonies the African population was deployed as forced labour – building railway networks and roads as well as being used to transport raw materials from the interior to the ports. The occupied countries were shamelessly exploited, as Africa's natural riches were shipped off to the mother countries of the colonial masters.

The European colonial powers employed a variety of methods in exercising their rule. Great Britain followed the principle of 'indirect rule' that it had already successfully practised in India. Leaving the traditional power structures in place and exploiting them to their own ends seemed a more efficient way of proceeding than summarily dispensing with all existing structures. After the First World War, the British colonial administrator Sir Frederick Lugard proclaimed indirect rule as an official doctrine. His 1922 work *The Dual Mandate in Tropical Africa* became the handbook of British colonial officers throughout the Empire. Other colonial powers, notably France, encouraged the implementation of direct governance by their colonial officers. In the tradition of the French Revolution of 1789, the country saw itself as the bearer of a civilisation whose values had universal applicability. The traditional structures were to be destroyed and replaced with French institutions. In principle, therefore, Senegal was as much a province of France as, say, Normandy. Yet this theory was never reflected in practice: at no time during French colonial rule in Africa did its subjects there enjoy even remotely the same rights as a French citizen in the 'mother country'.[37]

Regardless of whether they were guided by the principle of indirect or direct rule, throughout the continent the colonial masters resorted to repressive and indiscriminate measures to maintain their grip on power. For example, the propagandist of indirect rule Lord Lugard was perfectly well acquainted with other methods of rule. From 1900 to 1906 he served as British High Commissioner of the Northern Nigeria Protectorate. When, in 1906, the village of Satiru near the town of Sokoto rose up in rebellion, he ordered that it should be surrounded and all of its inhabitants shot. Some 2,000 unarmed men, women and children died in a hail of bullets fired from British Maxim guns.

'Heart of Darkness': The Belgian Congo

Nowhere did European colonialists conduct a more uninhibited and brutal rampage than in the Belgian-administered Congo. King Leopold II preached the virtues of civilisation but in practice brought barbarity. He transformed his Congo Free State into a country in which there was soon no free trade and no free citizens, only a monopolised economy and forced labour. All lands were declared to be state property. Hunting and fishing were deemed to be 'poaching', which was subject to the most draconian punishments. The result was a spate of famines that cost millions of Congolese their lives. The so-called Force Publique was feared throughout the country; this colonial army, commanded by Belgian officers, soon numbered over 17,000 recruits. It resembled a state-sponsored death squad more than a military unit. Its soldiers overran and sacked the villages of native people before burning them to the ground; they took women, children and old people hostage and kept them imprisoned in compounds where they had only the bare earth to sit on and nothing to eat. One of the principal tasks of the Force Publique was to raise punitive taxes from the population, payable in the form of supplies of natural rubber. There was good reason for this: the demand for natural rubber to be used in the manufacture of rubber products was huge in Europe and overseas, and the profit margins correspondingly enormous. In the Congo, anyone failing to deliver the specified quantities of the raw material had his or her hands cut off, or was shot dead. Alongside rubber, the cultivation of coffee and palm oil as well as the mining of copper, lead, zinc and diamonds all helped boost the Belgian king's coffers. In 1908, Leopold was forced to cede his personal colonial fiefdom to the Belgian state. Up to that date, his private empire had yielded him around $1.1 billion in profit, though he never set foot on African soil. In the process, he had presided over the eradication of fully half of 'his' Congolese subjects. The tyrannical rule of Belgium over the Congo is estimated to have cost the lives of around 10 million of its inhabitants –as a result of either massacre by the colonial army, forced labour and transportation or starvation.[38]

In his novel *Heart of Darkness*, written in 1899, the Polish-British novelist Joseph Conrad painted a startling and vivid picture of the atrocities being perpetrated in the Belgian Congo.[39] He knew what he was talking about, having travelled to the Congo as a merchant seaman some years previously. The central figure of the book is the unscrupulous colonialist Kurtz, who issues the order: 'Exterminate all the brutes!' This character was based on a real-life model: Léon Rom, a Belgian officer in the Force Publique. Rom had been responsible for countless massacres and 'punitive expeditions' against local tribal chiefs. In the garden of his colonial villa, he had the heads of 21 Congolese women displayed on spikes as ornaments in his flower borders. This dark period in the history of the Congo still resonates in the lives of the country's citizens. For instance, there is an idiom in the dialect of the Mongo people which translates literally as 'to send a person off to the rubber harvest', meaning to 'bully someone'.

Not just the Congo but also the colonies of other states attracted Europeans who were seeking to make a quick buck, and who neither feared risks nor entertained any scruples. 'Ship me somewhere east of Suez, where the best is like the worst / Where there aren't no Ten Commandments an' a man can raise a thirst', wrote Rudyard Kipling in his poem 'Mandalay'.[40] The whole of colonised Africa was one such region, where the Ten Commandments counted for little. The European commanders and their minions and sundry adventurers all left their bourgeois morality and Christian virtues back in their homelands. Even worse, in many instances they boasted of the atrocities they had committed and were decorated with medals for services rendered by their grateful governments back home.

First stirrings of resistance

It took some time for Africans to realise that it was not just a new order that their white conquerors had in mind. Many local rulers and chiefs believed in peaceful coexistence and counted on signing treaties with the Europeans. Once it dawned on them that colonialism was about the uprooting of their entire way of life, however, resistance began to grow right across the continent. While the Herero were staging their uprising in German South West Africa, the Maji Maji Revolt took the colonial regime in German East Africa by surprise in 1905.[41] There, several peoples banded together at the instigation of a religious leader called Kinjikitele, who prophesied that current conditions would be overturned and who acted as a lightning rod for the population's growing discontent. The introduction by the colonial authorities of a harsh poll tax proved to be the straw that broke the camel's back. Unrest broke out throughout the country; before long, over 20 different ethnic groups were involved in the insurrection. The rebels were eventually mowed down by the machine guns of the German 'Protection force' under the command of Theodor von Hassel. The fusillade from these deadly weapons left, in Hassel's words, 'rows, indeed mountains, of dead bodies' behind.[42] Even so, the African warriors did manage to tie the colonial troops down in a protracted guerrilla war that lasted several years. According to Tanzanian researchers, as many as 250,000 to 300,000 Africans perished in this conflict, while the number of deaths among the colonial forces amounted to just 15.[43]

In Rhodesia (modern Zimbabwe), some 20 years beforehand, the Ndebele and the Shona had risen up against Cecil Rhodes's British South Africa Company. While the revolt of the Ndebele collapsed after only a few months, the Shona put up resistance for several years. In Zululand in South Africa, the Zulu rose up against Boer settlers. Meanwhile, on the Côte d'Ivoire, the Baoulé people were involved in skirmishes with French colonists. In January 1915, in British Nyasaland (present-day Malawi), John Chilembwe, the pastor of a black Baptist community, led an uprising sparked by the colonial authorities' plan to conscript the native people of the region to fight against the German colonial army in the First World War. Chilembwe saw himself as the leader of a future African-run state. Soon after the start of the rebellion, though, he and most of his followers were killed by British colonial troops. Indeed, all these revolts and armed uprisings were ultimately put down by the troops of the colonial powers. Nevertheless, they turned out to be the precursors to many anticolonial wars of liberation in the twentieth century. Chilembwe, for example, is regarded as a folk hero in modern Malawi, with his portrait having been displayed on every denomination of banknote in the country.

The catalyst for many of these rebellions was the introduction of draconian taxes. 'If you pay taxes, then it means you have been defeated', runs a saying from Zimbabwe. The exploitation of African colonies followed a similar pattern everywhere. Fertile regions were covered in gigantic plantations growing produce for consumption in the 'mother countries', such as rubber, sisal, sugar, coffee, tea, tobacco, bananas, peanuts, palm oil and coconut oil. Small farmers were displaced onto barren tracts of land and were no longer able to grow sufficient food for themselves and their families. As a result, they hired themselves out as cheap labour on the European plantations. They were forced to purchase the food and goods sold by their colonial masters and pay for them with the money they earned. Over and above this, they were also required to pay a poll tax or hut tax – the revenue from which the Europeans used to fund their colonial regime. The traditional rulers and chiefs could do nothing to oppose this situation. A number of them even collaborated with the foreign rulers, a factor that further eroded their authority. What the people of colonised Africa experienced was nothing less than a Nietzschean 'revaluation of all values'.

Collaboration and cultural assimilation

Generally speaking, the colonial rulers set little store by the education of the indigenous population. In no other colonised country were there so few people attending school as in the Belgian Congo. Over all the years of Belgian rule, only seven native Congolese completed a course of university study; this handful included Patrice Lumumba, who subsequently became the first prime minister of an independent Congo. Even when a school was made available to the native populace, it was used to inculcate them with the 'values of western civilisation', teaching Eurocentric notions such as that the Gauls were their forebears. Ahmed Sékou Touré, the independence leader and later first president of Guinea, recalled his schooling in French West Africa:

> The books we read in the colonial schools taught us about the life of Joan of Arc and Napoleon, about the poetry of Lamartine and the plays of Molière, as if Africa had never had a history, or a past, or a geographical existence or a cultural life of its own. Our pupils were only accepted in so far as they demonstrated an ability to become completely assimilated culturally.[44]

Africans were expected to learn the language of their colonial masters, to wear European clothes and to adopt European manners. Their own cultures counted for nothing, and were seen as 'primitive' and a hindrance to progress; the religions of their parents were labelled idolatry. In this way, the very souls of Africans were also colonised.

Colonial schools, which were mostly set up under the aegis of the Christian missions, were at first viewed by many Africans with great suspicion. Muslims and adherents of traditional animistic religions feared that the intention was to divest them of their faith. Several rulers and chiefs preferred to send their slaves rather than the sons of influential families to the European schools. The first schools opened in Senegal and in French Sudan under the umbrella of the colonial administration were dubbed *écoles des otages* (hostage schools). The school established in Senegal later developed into the École William Ponty, which became a 'seedbed' for African nationalist movements.[45] Many of the independence leaders in West and Central Africa were educated here, including Félix Houphouët-Boigny, who later became the first president of Côte d'Ivoire, and Modibo Keïta, the first president of independent Mali.

Here and in the colonies of the other European powers, too, Africans came to see the education offered by the missions as an opportunity to improve their situation – albeit always under the conditions imposed by foreign rule. They understood that they would only be able to assert themselves against the whites if they began using their 'weapons'. Most of the founding fathers of African independence movements began their education by attending African mission schools, later going on to study at Western universities. Jomo Kenyatta, Kenya's first prime minister after the country gained independence from Britain, worked days at a general store in Nairobi and then took evening classes at a local Christian school. In the 1930s he was a student at the London School of Economics and Political

Science. Kwame Nkrumah, the leader of Ghana's independence movement and later the country's first president, attended the Catholic mission school in Half Assini, his father's hometown, as a child. He went on to study theology and economics at Lincoln University, Pennsylvania, and educational theory and philosophy at the University of Pennsylvania. The aforementioned father of Guinean independence, Ahmed Sékou Touré, went to a French technical college in Conakry, the capital of Guinea, and later worked for the French postal service, PTT.

The history of colonialism is also the history of collaboration. Africans got to know their colonial masters not just as oppressors but also as teachers, doctors, missionaries and engineers: they built roads, laid railway tracks, set up hospitals and constructed port facilities, dams and telegraph networks. They provided an educational system and established a bureaucracy. And many Africans entered – more or less willingly – into collaboration with the colonial administrators. But they were, and remained, toys to be manipulated by the foreign rulers. Europeans were very successful in playing various clans and ethnicities off against one another. It was tribalism that had allowed them to conquer and colonise Africa in the first place, and they now proceeded to govern their colonies according to the principle of 'divide and rule'.

Colonialism in decline

The First World War did not fundamentally disrupt the colonial system, although it did succeed in forcing one European colonial power to quit the African stage. Having lost the war, Germany fought a losing battle to retain its colonies. 'As a great civilisation, the German people have the right and the duty to collaborate in the scientific exploration of the world and in the education of undeveloped races,' the German government wrote in May 1919 in a communiqué to the victorious Allied powers.[46] Officially, Germany's colonies were placed under the administration of the newly established League of Nations, but for all practical purposes they were divided up among the victorious powers France, Great Britain and Belgium.

Parallel to the great Paris Peace Conference being held at the cessation of hostilities, a group of young African intellectuals gathered in Paris in 1919 for the first time to attend the inaugural Pan-African Congress, a forum for discussing how a future Africa might look without any foreign colonial control. 'Africans should take part in governing their countries as fast as their development permits,' ran the demand that the Congress presented to the peace conference, 'until, at some unspecified time in the future, Africa is granted home rule.' Their demand fell on deaf ears. The new world order that emerged in 1919 with the Treaty of Versailles, and the right of the peoples of the world to self-determination that was propagated by US President Woodrow Wilson, was evidently to have no purchase in Africa. In Europe after the First World War, democracies began to prevail, but in the eyes of the colonial masters, this was an unsuitable form of governance for Africa. Yet the idea of Pan-Africanism, of the unity of all African people irrespective of their ethnicity or nationality, was now out of the bottle.

The efflorescence of colonialism in the 1920s was brief and deceptive. The repercussions of the global economic crisis from 1930 onwards were felt in Africa too. The prices of raw materials that relied on world markets – such as coffee, cocoa, sugar cane and cotton – all collapsed. European nations resorted to an even more intensive exploitation of their colonies. Millions of Africans were plunged into destitution, and an increasing number of them agreed that the colonial system of coercion had to be brought to an end – once and for all.

The death knell for colonialism was struck by the outbreak of the Second World War. The US had no interest in supporting the colonial interests of their British allies in the struggle against Hitler's Germany. President Roosevelt stated that the right of peoples to self-determination should henceforth also apply in the colonies belonging to France and Great Britain. When the British Prime Minister Winston Churchill called for direct military support and arms from the US, Roosevelt made this dependent on two conditions: Great Britain had to agree to relinquish its colonies and allow the US a share in the trade in raw materials. On 14 August 1941, under the impact of the German invasion of the Soviet Union, Great Britain and the US signed the Atlantic Charter, which stated, among other provisions, that Great Britain and the US 'respect the right of all peoples to choose the form of Government under which they will live; and they wish to see sovereign rights and self-government restored to those who have been forcibly deprived of them'.[47] Five months previously, in May 1941, Emperor Haile Selassie, who had been driven from Ethiopia by the invasion of Mussolini's Fascist troops in 1935–36, had been restored to his throne; British troops had paved the way for his return by defeating the Italian occupation force. Could Churchill really have imagined that the Atlantic Charter's remit did not also extend to Britain's colonies in Africa and elsewhere?

It would be four more years before Hitler's Germany was finally brought to its knees. The US on one hand and the Soviet Union on the other became the key players in global politics. The year 1947 saw the passing by the British parliament of the Indian Independence Act, by which Great Britain 'released into independence' its colony of India. This marked the beginning of the end of the British Empire – and the end of European colonialism. Within a space of just three years, between 1946 and 1949, not only India and Pakistan but also Burma (Myanmar), Ceylon (Sri Lanka) and Indonesia gained their independence. It would not be long before the spark from Asia would jump over to Africa and ignite the independence movements there.

'We are determined to be free'

In October 1945, the heads of the African liberation movement gathered in Manchester for the Fifth Pan-African Congress. The participants included a series of men who would later go on to become the first presidents of their respective countries: Nnamdi Azikiwe (Nigeria), Kenneth Kaunda (Zambia), Jomo Kenyatta (Kenya), Kwame Nkrumah (Ghana), Julius Nyerere (Tanzania) and Ahmed Sékou Touré (Guinea). Their desire for fundamental change was reaffirmed in the closing declaration of the conference. 'We are determined to be free,' it proclaimed. 'We continue to sacrifice and strive. But we are unwilling to starve any longer while doing the world's drudgery, in order to support, by our poverty and ignorance, a false aristocracy and a discredited imperialism.'[48] But the declaration also contained a thinly veiled threat:

> The delegates to the Fifth Pan-African Congress believe in peace. How could it be otherwise when for centuries the African peoples have been victims of violence and slavery? Yet if the Western world is still determined to rule mankind by force, then Africans, as a last resort, may have to appeal to force in the effort to achieve Freedom, even if force destroys them and the world.

In many places, the path to independence would indeed turn out to be a bloody one, as the European powers did not want to let go of their colonies. Quite the contrary: Great Britain and France, which only recovered very slowly from the effects of the Second World War, accelerated the exploitation of their colonies. They hoped thereby to mobilise additional resources for rebuilding their economies. In effect, it was an attempt at a 'second colonisation'. But resistance against it could no longer be quelled. The chorus of voices grew ever louder, calling for armed struggle and rejecting any further cooperation with and accommodation of the colonial powers. In the British colony of Kenya in the early 1950s, the rural Kikuyu people launched a revolt against white farmers who had misappropriated their land. Their rebellion, which soon began to target British colonial officials and their supporters among the general populace, took on the characteristics of a civil war. The British dubbed it the 'Mau Mau Uprising' (the freedom fighters called themselves the Kenya Land and Freedom Army, but later adopted the British term, claiming it stood for Mzungu Aende Ulaya, Mwafrika Apate Uhuru – 'Let the foreigner go back abroad, let the African regain independence'). Even though the revolt was finally put down in 1956, pressure on the colonial powers kept growing. Great Britain sought to stave it off by granting its colonies greater autonomy.

France pursued quite a different course. Paris wanted to tie its colonies even more closely to the 'motherland'. As early as 1944, at the Brazzaville Conference, France had granted all of its colonies the right to send representatives to the French National Assembly (Senegal, or rather its so-called *quatre communes* of Dakar, Gorée, Saint-Louis and Rufisque, had already been doing so since the start of the twentieth century). Yet all these concessions availed the French nothing. The Afro-Asiatic

Conference held in 1955 in Bandung, Indonesia, had issued a final communiqué stating that 'colonialism in all its manifestations is an evil which should speedily be brought to an end'; this conference was also the catalyst for the formation of the Non-Aligned Movement.[49] The leaders of the independence movements in Africa and Asia, such as Nehru in India, Sukarno in Indonesia and Nasser in Egypt, were in close contact with one another and provided mutual support. As a result, more and more African states achieved their independence in the 1950s. This process began with Libya in 1951, followed in 1956 by Sudan, Morocco and Tunisia and thereafter Ghana and Guinea. In the 'Year of Africa' in 1960, no fewer than 18 colonies in Africa secured their independence: British Somaliland and Italian Somaliland, Cameroon, Togo, Madagascar, the Democratic Republic of Congo, the Republic of Dahomey (Benin), Niger, Upper Volta, Côte d'Ivoire, Chad, the Central African Republic, the Republic of Congo, Gabon, Senegal, Mali, Nigeria and Mauritania. Sierra Leone and Tanganyika (Tanzania) followed in 1961, and a year later Algeria, Uganda, Rwanda and Burundi.

One of the most horrific wars of independence was fought in Algeria. France was determined to hold onto its colony at all costs – no doubt partly because a million French settlers were resident in the country, and made up at least 12 per cent of the total population of Algeria at that time. In 1954, Ahmed Ben Bella – who later became Algeria's first president – announced the formation of the National Liberation Front (FLN), a cadre organisation on the model of communist states, which embarked on an armed struggle against the colonial regime. The FLN presently began receiving assistance from other African states that had already won their independence. France sent 400,000 troops to try and put down the revolt.

Fighting alongside them were the French-Algerians, the so-called *pieds-noirs*. Although they succeeded in defeating the FLN they failed to restore peace to the country. After a long series of negotiations, the French president Charles de Gaulle finally recognised Algerian independence on 18 March 1962 in the Évian Accords. However, Algeria only finally gained full sovereignty of the Algerian Sahara region in 1968, prior to which time the area had been used by France for atomic weapons testing.

The first European colonists were also the last to leave. Under its long-time dictator António Salazar, Portugal fought tooth-and-nail to retain its African colonies of Angola, Guinea-Bissau, Cape Verde and Mozambique, along with São Tomé and Príncipe. Portugal's war against the African independence movements that grew up in these regions went on for 10 years. It was brutal and costly and finally resulted in a coup being staged in the motherland to topple the Salazar regime in 1974. In 1975, the newly democratic government of Portugal recognised the independence of its colonies. In 1980, white rule also came to an end in Rhodesia (named after the British–South African colonialist Cecil Rhodes), and Robert Mugabe was installed as the president of the new state of Zimbabwe. South Africa – with its apartheid regime that had increasingly become an international pariah – and its occupied territory of Namibia thus became the last places in Africa to withhold the right of self-determination from the overwhelming majority of their citizens.

In newly independent Africa, it was not a question of starting again from scratch. Certainly, in many places, the departing colonial masters implemented a scorched-earth policy. The Portuguese demolished their villas in Maputo and Luanda, while the French destroyed the infrastructure of Guinea. As they rolled up their flags, ready to leave, their thinking was clearly: 'Let the ungrateful Africans see how well they cope on their own.' But the end of the colonial period did not mean a return to precolonial conditions. Now that they were finally masters of their own countries, Africans had no intention of giving up the infrastructure – municipal facilities, schools, law courts, railway networks, mines, companies and currencies – that the colonial powers had put in place, but instead were keen to take it over and develop it further. All these things were acquisitions that no African leader wanted to do without.

In some countries, prior to their withdrawal, the former colonial powers had managed to install sympathetic client regimes or at least to secure their investments. Thus, for example, Belgium ensured that its state shares in mines, plantations and factories were not nationalised by the new independent states but were transferred to a newly founded joint Belgian-Congolese development corporation. 'I felt like a cowboy from a Western who keeps on getting cleaned out by professional swindlers,' recalled Joseph Mobutu – later head of state and dictator of Zaïre (the Democratic Republic of Congo) – who took part in the negotiations in Brussels that paved the way for the country's independence. 'Through a whole series of legalistic and hard-headed sophistries, our opposite numbers in the talks managed to ensure that multinationals and Belgian capitalists maintained their firm grip on the Congo's commercial portfolio.'[50]

Nor did it end there. When the first democratically elected prime minister of the Congo, Patrice Lumumba, attempted to nationalise Belgian-owned mining concerns and plantations, and started to make overtures to the Soviet Union, Belgium openly colluded in his overthrow. On 17 January 1961 Lumumba fell victim to an assassination engineered by the Belgian secret service, the CIA and local conspirators. He was shot dead in the presence of Belgian officers.[51] Eventually, Mobutu – previously the army's chief of staff – came to power; he was able to count on the support of the United States. He rechristened the country Zaïre, from an indigenous word for the River Congo, and changed his own name to Mobutu Sese Seko Nkuku wa za Banga (meaning 'the all-powerful warrior who because of his endurance and inflexible will to win will go from conquest to conquest leaving fire in his wake'). Mobutu would turn out to be one of the worst despots in the history of Africa.

A similar picture unfolded in most of the new African states, which had been precipitated headlong into independence. The new rulers of their countries were young, inexperienced and ill-prepared for their roles as ministers, provincial governors, police chiefs, army commanders, banking presidents and senior judges. Nevertheless, people's expectations and hopes for the independent nations were enormous. 'Tomorrow we will be the USA: the United States of Africa!' declared Kwame Nkrumah at the end of the 1950s. In 1963, at a meeting in the Ethiopian capital Addis Ababa, the Organisation of African Unity (OAU) was established, including all independent African states. The OAU affirmed the state borders that had been set by the colonial powers – African leaders were too afraid to open the Pandora's box of tribalism, which had since time immemorial always represented the greatest danger to the continent. The European nations had only managed to conquer Africa thanks to tribalism, by playing off one ethnicity against another. Now the African founding fathers bent all their efforts towards building up African nation-states with national identities. They imported the European idea of a nation-state in order to overcome the African tendency to tribal thinking. 'You are not an Ibo now,' ran the modern orthodoxy, 'but a

Nigerian' – 'You are a Kenyan rather than a Kikuyu,' and so on. Everything was staked on the institution of central governments, without taking account of the fact that, with the sole exception of Somalia, all African countries are characterised by a multiethnic society, with a corresponding multiplicity of different ways of life, languages and religions. (It is an irony of history that, of all places, the only African country with one racial grouping, one language and one religion should have disintegrated in the 1990s, with rival clans seizing the reins of power.) By the same virtue, the African founding fathers at their conference in Addis Ababa also rejected Nkrumah's idea of a unitary African parliament; for the foreseeable future, then, there was to be no United States of Africa.

A feeling of a new departure gripped the entire continent. Most people were convinced that for Africa, finally liberated from the yoke of colonialism, a new golden era was dawning. And weren't the prospects for that very bright indeed? In the year of its independence, the GDP of Ghana was twice that of South Korea, while its per-capita income was as high as Spain's. The country was the world's largest cocoa producer and had considerable diamond and gold deposits. Throughout the continent, according to Africans' expectations, mineral wealth in the form of gold, silver, platinum and cobalt would now be exploited for the common good, together with the trade in agricultural produce – coffee, cocoa, sugar, bananas, peanuts, tropical hardwoods and much more besides. At independence, the Congo was at a more advanced stage of industrialisation than Brazil. It had access to railway lines, roads and maritime transport. In Nigeria, many workers could afford to buy a Volkswagen, while the country generously extended development aid to less well-off neighbouring states. Not just in Africa but globally, too, there was a general belief that Africa was the coming continent of the near future and that emergent African nations would before long be able to open their markets to the industrialised nations of the West. No one at that stage spoke about the Asian 'tiger economies' – rather, it was the 'lion states' of Africa that seemed about to pounce.

African administrations were determined to position themselves at the cutting edge of modernisation. In Ghana, after a construction period lasting five years, the largest dam in the world was inaugurated in 1966. The gigantic Volta Dam was primarily intended to supply electricity for the country's aluminium-smelting industry. Kenya planned to develop a home-produced automobile, while in Zaïre Mobutu – with the support of the German company Orbital Transport and Rockets (OTRAG) – even sought to develop his own missile technology.[52]

Squandering independence

For a while there was much to suggest that these ambitious plans might well come to fruition: in the 1960s and 1970s, many African countries such as Zaïre, Gabon and Cameroon achieved annual growth rates of 10 per cent and more. But before long, the key design flaw in the concept of independent African states became apparent. Not only did the new rulers lack technical know-how, but with the passage of time it became clear that they also lacked the will to improve general standards of living in their countries. And above all, there was a dearth of democratic institutions on which to build. The former colonial masters had had no interest in developing and promoting these. At the time of independence, very few African states had a functioning multiparty parliamentary system. By contrast, in the Congo there were so many mutually hostile parties and factions that there was no question of forming a stable government – and this served as a discouraging example to many other African nations.

Moreover, most of the leaders of the independence movements, who considered themselves revolutionaries and so leant towards the Soviet Union, actually saw absolutely no need for a multiparty arrangement, an independent judiciary and a system of checks and balances. They derived their ruling legitimacy from having liberated their countries – and laid claim to this right to rule for life. Consequently, a whole series of one-party states with an authoritarian figure at their head came into existence – for example, Sékou Touré in Guinea and Mobutu in Zaïre. They saw the expression of the will of the people embodied in their person. Elections were considered a tiresome and necessary evil, and when they were held, they were seen at best as a way of confirming and consolidating the leader's position.

The new rulers converted the movements that had put them in control into power apparatuses that helped them maintain their dictatorial rule. The opposition was harassed and suppressed. The new African elites were primarily concerned with feathering their own nests. They acquired expensive limousines and villas and vied with one another to see how much champagne they could consume – and in so doing simply perpetuated the privileged existence of their former European rulers. They regarded revenue from exports as their private income, and presently ceased to give any thought to their populaces and their standard of living. Corruption was omnipresent, affecting all levels of administration from the highest echelons of government right down to local officials and policemen in the remotest of regions. The primary aim of the new ruling cliques was to retain power, and this was secured by a system of patronage. Their own clans and members of their own ethnic group were given sinecures, while their home regions were showered with lavish financial support and their administrative staffs bloated to the point of inefficiency. The colonial masters had shown them the way, and now they slipped readily into their role and started to behave like their erstwhile oppressors. Frantz Fanon, the Martinique-born pioneer of decolonisation, got to the heart of the matter with his phrase *'peau noire, masques blancs'* ('black skin, white masks').[53]

The former colonial masters in Europe were largely untroubled by the new African kleptocracies, indeed quite the opposite. The new rulers often maintained friendly contact with the former colonial powers, and the latter pursued their own geopolitical interests. African countries became pawns in the strategic machinations of the Cold War. The two great power blocs vied to exert their influence in Africa. Regardless of whether it was in Moscow, Beijing, Washington or Paris, no expense was spared in wooing potential alliance partners with injections of hard cash or, where necessary, with missiles and tanks as well. The United States and its allies were just as indifferent as the USSR and its socialist 'brother nations' to whether the client states they were supporting were democratically organised or not. Administrations in Washington, London and Paris were equally adept at turning a blind eye where human rights and democratic structures were concerned. When US secretary of state Cordell Hull once complained to President Franklin Roosevelt that the US was supporting dictatorships in South America, and told him that they were 'all bastards', Roosevelt is reputed to have replied: 'Yes, I know they're bastards, but at least they're our bastards.' This dictum found a new lease of life in Africa, with Western and Soviet leaders propping up their own pet dictators. France was a prime example. When Jean-Bédel Bokassa, the ruler of the

Central African Republic – one of the poorest countries on the continent – had himself crowned emperor on 4 December 1977, the former colonial power sent him as a gift a two-tonne gilded throne and a crown studded with 2,000 diamonds. After coming to power in a coup d'état staged over the new year of 1965–66, Bokassa's first acts were to annul the constitution and execute several hundred political opponents. Yet so long as the dictator was prepared to do France's bidding, the administration in Paris generously overlooked all the human rights abuses Bokassa committed. When he was finally toppled in 1979, France readily granted the dictator political asylum.

Military strongmen

However, the original African founding fathers did not succeed in clinging on to power everywhere. Corruption, megalomania and nepotism combined to undermine their legitimacy to govern, and the more memories of the glorious days of liberation faded, the more people came out in opposition to the new injustices. In many African countries, the army was the only efficiently run institution. Their hour now arrived. African officers exploited the general atmosphere of discontent and organised coups against the aging heads of state. In many places, the new rulers were greeted enthusiastically by the populace and great hopes were invested in them – such as in Ghana, where President Kwame Nkrumah, who had led his country to independence, was deposed by the military while making a state visit abroad. This event would mark the beginning of a period of instability for Ghana. Over the subsequent 15 years, four further military coups took place. Finally, in 1981, flight lieutenant Jerry Rawlings seized power and ruled the country as a dictator for the next 20 years.

In 1974, Ethiopian army officers toppled the government of Emperor Haile Selassie. Here too, many people hoped that the young officers would bring Africa what it so badly needed: democratic institutions and a free-market economy. They were to be bitterly disappointed. The country's new rulers turned to the Soviet Union, and Colonel Mengistu Haile Mariam installed a regime of 'Red Terror'. According to estimates by Amnesty International, during Mengistu's 17-year rule, more than 100,000 Ethiopians were imprisoned and tortured and tens of thousands were murdered.[54] Other agencies have estimated that as many as 200,000 were killed.

Following Ethiopia's example, several other coup leaders turned their eyes towards the Eastern Bloc: capitalism was not for Africa, they claimed, and they sought salvation in socialism instead. One person who went his own way was Julius Nyerere, who had led Tanganyika into independence from Great Britain in 1961 and was elected president the following year. Following unification with the island of Zanzibar in 1964, he became president of the new country of Tanzania. Like many other socialist-influenced African heads of state, he presided over a one-party state and nationalised banks and commercial enterprises. Even though his efforts were not crowned with great economic success, he did set great store by education. Between 1960 and 1979, the country's rate of literacy increased from 10 to 79 per cent. Yet his Ujamaa project (Swahili for 'village community'), a massive relocation plan, turned into a fiasco. The rural population of Tanzania was induced – more or less voluntarily – to move to newly built village settlements, each housing 2,000 inhabitants. Nyerere believed that this figure constituted the ideal unit for a socialist community. By the end of the 1970s, over 60 per cent of the rural population of Tanzania had been resettled in these communities, most of which lacked even the most basic amenities. Anyone who had the wherewithal beat a hasty retreat from the settlements and built themselves a hut far away from the Ujamaa villages. When he stepped down from office in 1985, Nyerere left behind a bankrupt country. However, he must be credited with one thing: he was determined to lead by example and, unlike most of the other African potentates, lived very modestly. He used a Volkswagen Beetle as his official state car. Furthermore, after having acknowledged the failure of his policies to himself and the wider world, he took it upon himself to stand down from the office of president. No one had ever witnessed such a thing in Africa. Elsewhere the principle 'once in power, always in power' applied, and a ruler's term in office could only be brought to an end through a military takeover or a popular uprising. It was difficult, Nyerere is reputed to have said on stepping down, to build socialism in a country where there was only one socialist.

As a rule, African countries showed little concern for what was going on within the borders of others. People ruled according to the motto 'don't get involved in other countries' affairs'. All that changed in 1979, however. In April of that year, a combined force of the Tanzanian army and Ugandan rebel groups marched into Kampala, the capital of Uganda, in order to depose the dictator Idi Amin – who had been chief of the army general staff in Uganda when he seized power by means of a coup in January 1971. In 1976 he proclaimed himself president for life. He proceeded to plunge one of Africa's most prosperous countries into misery and chaos. He went down in history as the 'butcher of Africa': according to some estimates, as many as 500,000 Ugandans fell victim to his violent rule.[55] One of the major reasons he managed to cling on to power for many years was because Western governments supported him and the Soviet Union supplied him with arms. When, in the autumn of 1978, he ordered his forces to invade neighbouring Tanzania, and thereby threatened to destabilise the entire region, the Tanzanian army, in conjunction with the liberation force the Uganda National Liberation Army (UNLA), which was made up of Ugandan exiles, launched a counteroffensive that eventually forced Idi Amin into exile. He would finally find refuge in Saudi Arabia, where he died in 2003.

Uganda, in its turn, descended into civil war, which only ended when the rebel army led by Yoweri Museveni captured Kampala in 1986. Ever since then, up to the time of writing, Museveni has presided over the country with no sign whatsoever that he will step down voluntarily from his position. He specifically altered the constitution in order be able to stay in power for longer. He was re-elected president in February 2016 with over 60 per cent of the vote. Museveni is fond of pointing out that a third of the seats in the Ugandan parliament are reserved for women, along with five for young people and five for the disabled.[56] Yet there is no functioning party system, and Museveni's only serious political challenger, Kizza Besigye, has repeatedly been arrested and detained. The passing of a law in 2014 threatening homosexuals with lifelong imprisonment sparked international outrage. In defiance of protests worldwide, Museveni went ahead and ratified this piece of legislation. Nonetheless, he continues to be regarded as an ally of the West, with the US alone sending Uganda around €300 million in aid every year.[57]

The wind of change

The fall of the Iron Curtain in 1989–90 fostered hopes of democratic change throughout the world. Moscow's satellite regimes in Africa duly crumbled, including Mengistu Haile

Mariam's bloody tyranny in Ethiopia. For the time being, the country had outlived its geopolitical usefulness on the chessboard of East–West confrontation. And, finally, the apartheid regime in South Africa also came to an end. At the beginning of 1990, South Africa withdrew from South West Africa, ending a century of foreign rule there, and in March of that year the latter country gained its independence as the state of Namibia. The white minority government of F. W. de Klerk entered into negotiations on a democratic South Africa with representatives of organisations advocating majority rule, including the ANC leader Nelson Mandela, released after spending 27 years in gaol. In 1994, these talks culminated in the first free elections in South Africa and the installation of Nelson Mandela as the country's first democratically elected president.

The wind of change blew through many countries at this time, and the clamour among African populations for democratic representation grew ever louder. Yet rather than the creation of new, properly functioning political systems, all too often the result was only more confusion and uncertainty. Liberia descended into civil war. Somalia became a failed state and Central Africa was transformed into killing fields. When Mobutu was finally toppled from power in Zaïre in 1978, a new strongman was already waiting in the wings. The rebel leader Laurent Kabila restored the country's original name of the Congo and cast about for new allies. Whereas the main beneficiaries of Mobutu's regime had been Belgian, French and South African concerns like the multinational De Beers mining company, Kabila now guaranteed American companies preferential trading arrangements. Thus, the American Mineral Fields (AMF) concern acquired the majority of the copper and cobalt mines of the Kolwezi region for the bargain price of $1 billion – only around one-tenth of their estimated total value.[58]

The people to benefit from the country's mineral wealth were diamond dealers, commodity traders, international consortia and the Congo's ruling cliques, while the general populace were left empty-handed – and nothing has since changed to improve this situation.

Alongside corruption, the tendency towards centralisation, which the founding fathers of African independence inherited from their erstwhile colonial masters, proved to be a curse for the continent. In many countries, centralisation only succeeded in stirring up opposition from liberation movements representing various different ethnicities, who presently sought (and in many cases are still seeking) to obtain their independence by force of arms. This was also the case in Ethiopia, which declared itself to be an 'ethnic federation' and divided itself into a number of regions along ethnic lines. This process has gone so far that on Ethiopian identity cards nowadays the holder's 'race' is given – Tigray, Amhara and so on. Where such a development can lead was shown at the beginning of the 1990s in Rwanda, when the Hutu launched murderous attacks on the country's Tutsi population. The roots of this genocide, which cost the lives of over 800,000 Tutsi, go back to colonial times. When Belgium took over Rwanda from German control at the end of the First World War, the colonial masters, true to the principle of 'divide and rule', showed clear favouritism towards the Tutsi, whom they classed as a superior ethnicity as a result of their relative prosperity, while the Hutu were regarded as a 'lower-order race'. Before long they began to assess the indigenous population and to assign them to one or the other ethnicity. Any Rwandan who owned more than twelve cattle was categorised henceforth as a Tutsi. Their ethnic classification was even included on their passports. Decades later, this categorisation along ethnic lines by the colonial power was to have disastrous consequences. 'The seeds of genocide were sown when the Belgians introduced identity cards,' Rwanda's president Paul Kagame stated in 2007.[59]

Certainly, after decades of independence it would be wrong to try and blame the former colonial powers for all of Africa's ills. For many of Africa's leaders this remains to the present day an all-too-convenient excuse. Even so, the legacy of colonialism does continue to hinder development in Africa in many respects. For one thing, there are the demarcation lines that were drawn in the continent by the colonial powers, and which are often downright absurd. Take, for example, Nigeria, which is a wholly artificial entity with three major peoples – the Yoruba, the Iba and the Hausa/Fulani – and 430 smaller ethnicities, which seriously hampers development there. As one seasoned Africa correspondent, Bartholomäus Grill, has put it: 'The British midwives cast an evil spell over Nigeria when they assisted at its birth.'[60] Likewise, the agricultural monocultures introduced by the colonial powers, which were geared to producing maximum profit, meant that many African countries remained dependent upon the export of a handful of primary goods – say, coffee from Uganda and cocoa from Côte d'Ivoire. When the global market price for raw materials and farm produce fell, it plunged these nations into crisis. Especially since they also lacked the money to pay the increased cost of industrial goods and energy that they were obliged to import.

Equally fallacious is an attitude that clings on tenaciously in the West: namely, that 50 years of postcolonial Africa have shown that Africans are wholly incapable of governing their own affairs. Anyone looking at the long list of postcolonial dictators – from Bokassa in the Central African Republic/ Empire and Mengistu Haile Mariam in Ethiopia, through Idi Amin in Uganda and Siad Barre in Somalia, to Hissène Habré in Chad – might well feel vindicated in taking such a view. Yet this would be to ignore the fact that almost all these dictators would not have been able to remain in power for long if they had not been propped up by their powerful allies in the East and West.

The hope that things would fundamentally change after the collapse of the Soviet Union was only short-lived. The disastrous tendency on the part of developed nations to search out alliance partners regardless of how despotically they ruled their own people soon gained a new lease of life – most notably from 2001 onwards, following the terror attacks of 9/11 that shook the Western world. What were once the 'pet dictators' of the great power blocs are now their 'partners in the War on Terror'. 'As long as you stand shoulder-to-shoulder with me in the fight against Islamic State,' the mantra runs, 'you can do what you like to your own populace.' Even the former European colonial powers, first and foremost France and Great Britain, have not ceased to try and secure their spheres of influence.

Almost all of the former architects of African independence have now stepped down. Only Isaias Afewerki continues to govern in Eritrea, and the aged Robert Mugabe was only recently ousted as Zimbabwe's head of state. They too have their place in the rogues' gallery of African despots. In Zimbabwe a kleptocratic state has long attempted to safeguard its ill-gotten wealth by compelling sectors of its populace to work as forced labourers in its diamond fields, watched over by the Zimbabwean army. In 2010 the whistle-blowing website Wikileaks published confidential US documents which revealed that Mugabe, together with his wife and senior government officials, had amassed huge personal fortunes from the illegal trade in diamonds from the Chiadzwa mine.[61] Yet, while this was going on, President Mugabe continued to rail against the corruption of the West with monotonous regularity. Time will tell whether the advent in November 2017 of the new president, Emmerson Mnangagwa – a protégé and right-hand-man of Mugabe – will have an impact on corruption, and whether Mnangagwa will develop constructive or contradictory relationships with European states. After all, the honorary doctorates bestowed on Mugabe by Western universities were all revoked in the latter years of his presidency, but the West continued to shore up Mugabe's regime year after year with around $350 million in development aid.[62]

'The colonizer, who in order to ease his conscience gets into the habit of seeing the other man as an animal, accustoms himself to treating him like an animal, and tends objectively to transform himself into an animal,' wrote the Martinique-born Aimé Césaire – one of the founders of the Négritude movement, which promoted the cultural self-determination of all Africans – wrote in 1950. He went on:

> They talk to me about progress, about "achievements," diseases cured, improved standards of living. I am talking about societies drained of their essence, cultures trampled underfoot [...] thousands of men sacrificed [...] I am talking about millions of men in whom fear has been cunningly instilled, who have been taught to have an inferiority complex, to tremble, kneel, despair, and behave like flunkeys.[63]

It has taken a long time for the European colonial powers to acknowledge their responsibility and to begin to process their colonial history. It was a hundred years before Germany officially admitted to the crimes it had perpetrated against the Herero in German South West Africa. In July 2015, the Foreign Ministry in Berlin finally brought itself to issue the following statement: 'The war of annihilation conducted in Namibia from 1904 to 1908 was a war crime and an act of genocide.'[64] The atrocities committed by Belgian colonists in the Congo have entered into the Belgian public consciousness in recent years; the subject has only really been openly discussed since around 2000. To date, Italy has never officially apologised for the war crimes it committed, including its use of poison gas during its invasion of Ethiopia in 1935–36 and its subsequent five-year-long occupation of the country. Right up to the late 1990s, the French took great exception to the phrase 'Algerian War', still so deeply ingrained was the conviction that this African country had been an integral part of France.[65] It was only in 1999 that the French National Assembly officially approved the use of the term. Similarly, Great Britain is still reluctant to engage with the darker aspects of its colonial history. When will the Western world finally begin to face up to its responsibilities and draw the appropriate conclusions?

Whether they like it or not, the fact remains that colonialism is what brought Africa and Europe together. If one lesson can be drawn from these centuries of shared history, it is this: the common future of the neighbouring continents of Europe and Africa can only reside in a cooperative partnership with one another. And the basis for this relationship must necessarily be those values of which the West is so rightly proud to be the progenitor: human rights, democracy and the rule of law.

3

AFRICA IS ALWAYS GOOD
FOR A SURPRISE

Africa has a poor image in the wider world. For people in Europe or in other industrialised regions, thinking of Africa immediately conjures up images of violence, poverty and disease. They still have in their minds' eye the television pictures of famine disasters that have, time and again since the 1970s, been broadcast around the world: children who are nothing but skin and bone, with stick-like legs and their stomachs distended by the effects of kwashiorkor (severe malnutrition). Starving men and women squatting on the bare earth, staring blankly out of hollowed eye sockets, with their hair desiccated or falling out. Clouds of flies on the faces of people too weak to shoo them away. In recent times, these long-familiar images have been joined by new ones: long processions of emaciated people crossing the desert carrying all their worldly possessions, which in most cases consist of nothing more than a backpack, or hundreds of people crammed onto an inflatable boat cast adrift and abandoned to their fate on the vast blue expanse of the ocean.

These are images of real events, and yet at the same time they are clichés. For modern Africa also consists of booming metropolises, economies with annual growth rates in double figures, thriving commercial concerns and, at the current count, some 163,000 millionaires. 'If someone starts talking

to me and I tell them I come from Africa,' says the successful British-Nigerian female entrepreneur Ola Orekunrin,
'all Europeans suddenly declare they want to save me – no
matter whether they are shoeshine boys or waiters. Why do
they always think I need saving?'[66] The 31-year-old Orekunrin, who was born and brought up in London, belongs to that
generation who are mindful of their roots and see their future
in Africa. She studied for her degree in medicine in England
and, at the age of 21, became one of the youngest graduates
ever in the country. Thereafter, she worked for some years as
a doctor in the UK and trained as a helicopter pilot. During a
trip to Nigeria, she decided to relocate to her parents' country
of origin. In Lagos she founded Flying Doctors Nigeria, the
first private air ambulance service in the country, with its own
fleet of helicopters. She was adamant, she says, that she wanted
to set up a private enterprise with a profit motive rather than
an aid agency because she did not want to be reliant on international aid resources and donations. At the World Economic
Forum in 2014, Orekunrin was inducted into the circle of
Young Global Leaders. She points to Africa's women, who are
on the rise throughout the continent, founding law chambers
and businesses, entering parliaments and assuming ministerial responsibilities. Africa can even boast two female heads of
state: Ellen Johnson Sirleaf, who has been president of Liberia
since 2006 and whose campaigning for women's rights won her
the Nobel Peace Prize in 2011, and Joyce Banda, who was president of Malawi from 2012 to 2014.

'Lions on the move'

'*Ex Africa semper aliquid novi*,' the Roman writer Pliny the
Elder is reputed to have said some 2,000 years ago – 'there's

always something new coming from Africa'; it's always good for a surprise. Africa comprises, on the one hand, vast rural areas where things have scarcely changed for centuries, and, on the other hand, rapidly booming cities with all their excesses. Many Africans like Orekunrin face the future full of confidence, and pour all their energies into securing the future of the continent. Their optimism is not without foundation: in many regions of Africa, the free market economy is on the up and up. 'Lions on the Move' was the title that the American consultancy group McKinsey gave to its 2010 report on Africa.[67] Since the turn of the millennium, almost all African economies have developed strongly, with annual growth rates of between 5 and 10 per cent. Even in 2008 the continent's GDP of US $1.6 billion was higher than that of Russia or Brazil, while by 2014 the figure had increased to US $2.4 billion. Economic reforms played a part: in many countries borrowings and budget deficits were cut, inflation kept in check, state-owned industries privatised and trade liberalised.

The boom in the energy sector and the huge worldwide demand for raw materials and minerals helped fuel the upturn in Africa. According to figures issued by the African Union, 38 per cent of the world's deposits of uranium, 73 per cent of platinum, 88 per cent of diamonds and 42 per cent of gold are found in Africa. The continent also had 80 per cent of known coltan deposits, 57 per cent of cobalt, 39 per cent of manganese, 31 per cent of phosphates and 9 per cent of the world's bauxite reserves.[68] In countries such as Mozambique, Angola and Namibia, oil is the economy's principal driver. Off the coast of Ghana, Liberia and Sierra Leone there are also huge oil deposits, which form the basis of optimistic economic projections by the governments of those countries. The former Portuguese colony of Angola, for example, has experienced unprecedented growth over the last 10 years as a result of its oil wealth. After independence in 1975, a bitter civil war raged in Angola and only came to an end in 2002, by which time the conflict had brought the country to its knees. Over the years that followed, though, Angola posted one economic growth record after another, with annual rates of up to 18 per cent. In 2013, Angola achieved a GDP of $124 billion, while its annual per-capita income was almost $6,000. In a ranking of the world's most expensive cities prepared by the consultancy firm Mercer, the Angolan capital Luanda was in second place below Hong Kong, surpassing such places as Zurich, Singapore and Tokyo.[69] The monthly rental cost of an average two-bedroom apartment in the centre of this city of seven million inhabitants was some $6,700. Oil was the driving force behind this soaring growth: in 2013 alone, Angola earned around $60 billion in revenue from the export of oil.[70] This new-found prosperity even put Angola in a position to extend credit to its former colonial master Portugal, which was suffering the effects of the worldwide financial crisis that began in 2008. Yet, despite the boom, half of all Luanda's citizens still live in slums that have no electricity or mains water supply.

The former French colony Côte d'Ivoire is another example of this sea change. Even just a few years ago, the country was numbered among the continent's most hopeless economic cases. In the presidential elections at the end of 2010, the opposition leader Alassane Ouattara and the incumbent Laurent Gbagbo engaged in a bitter battle over who had won the ballot. The constitutional crisis escalated into a civil war. Many people were murdered, many businesses – including branches of international concerns – were looted and public order broke down. By the end of March 2011, a million people had been displaced. Finally, the old colonial power France intervened in the conflict and managed to pacify the country. Within the space of just a few years, the economy recovered from the upheaval of the civil war. Today, Côte d'Ivoire is the strongest member of the West African Economic and Monetary Union (UEMOA) and, with a growth rate of 8.4 per cent, the country was second only to Ethiopia as the Africa's fastest-growing economy in 2015.

A continent of 1.2 billion opportunities

However, the global financial crisis of 2008–9 did not leave Africa entirely unscathed. Throughout the world, the prices of raw materials plummeted, and the effects of this were felt in Johannesburg, Lagos and Luanda. The growth rates of oil-producing countries like Algeria, Angola, Nigeria and Sudan fell. In 2016, Angola posted a growth rate of just 0.6 per cent and a per-capita income of $3,500.[71] In addition, the political upheavals caused by the Arab Spring uprisings in the countries of North Africa also had a knock-on effect in economic terms: the economies of Egypt, Libya and Tunisia showed no growth in the period between 2010 and 2015. Yet, much to the astonishment of many observers, Africa weathered the storm of the global economic crisis better than elsewhere: on average, the economies of Africa grew by 4.4 per cent annually between 2010 and 2015 – a figure that was roughly on a par with that for the period 2005–2010. Over the same period, productivity increased by 1.7 per cent (in comparison with 1.6 per cent annually for 2000–2010).[72] Moreover, economists around the world continued to judge Africa's ongoing economic prospects as being bright. In 2000, *The Economist* talked in terms of 'Hopeless Africa', whereas in 2016 the same magazine rhapsodised about the continent of '1.2 billion opportunities':

Africa's 1.2 billion people also hold plenty of promise. They are young: south of the Sahara, their median age is below 25 everywhere except in South Africa. They are better educated than ever before: literacy rates among the young now exceed 70% [...] They are richer: in sub-Saharan Africa, the proportion of people living on less than $1.90 a day fell from 56% in 1990 to 35% in 2015, according to the World Bank. And diseases that have ravaged life expectancy and productivity are being defeated – gradually for HIV and AIDS, but spectacularly for malaria.[73]

McKinsey also identified driving forces for a sustained economic boom in the growing young population, urbanisation and development of new technologies. Africa is seen as one of the last virtually untapped markets in the world. In line with this, the German-African Business Association wrote in its study of business trends for Africa up to the year 2025:

Africa is the last continent on Earth that – except in South Africa and some countries of North Africa – has not experienced industrialisation in a Western sense [...] It is no longer a question of whether Africa, leaving aside the production of raw materials, will ever compete in the global economic market, but when.

This same body drew the conclusion that 'Africa is a sleeping giant. And that giant is just about to wake up'.[74] Africa is currently home to around 700 major concerns, many of which now operate right across the continent. Taken together, they generate some $1.4 billion and many of them – especially in the energy transport and health sectors – are on course to expand.[75] Over the past 10 years, sales of new cars alone have increased by half. In many sectors of the economy, the growth rates are enormous.

'Get out there!': investment in Africa

These trends have not gone unnoticed by investors around the globe. In 2004, foreign direct investments in Africa totalled $14 billion, and by 2014 these had already increased to $73 billion. In 2012, Coca-Cola and Unilever registered more than 10 per cent of their worldwide sales in Africa. In the summer of 2014, Jeffrey Immelt, then chairman of the board of General Electric, stated that 'Africa is one of the most important growth areas, purely from an economic standpoint'. This American energy giant announced that by year-end 2018 it would invest a total of €1.5 billion in Africa.[76]

The largest investor in Africa has in fact been the People's Republic of China. In 1996 Beijing proclaimed the new economic strategy of *zou chu qu* ('get out there!'), and the effects of this new spirit of outward investment were felt particularly strongly in Africa. Within two decades, China increased its trade with the continent from $1 billion in 1992 to $210 billion in 2013. According to figures issued by the Chinese trade ministry, by 2014 the country's investments in Africa amounted to $32 billion, representing a 20-fold increase within the space of a decade.[77] During this period, more than 2,000 Chinese companies began operating within Africa, while the number of joint Chinese-African projects has gone beyond the 8,000 mark. The Chinese are opening up oilfields in Angola, investing in copper extraction in Zambia and undertaking mining operations in the Democratic Republic of Congo, Ghana and Zimbabwe. They are heavily involved in agriculture and hold billions of dollars' worth of shares in Africa's largest bank, the

Standard Bank of South Africa. They have built roads, port installations, dams, hospitals, airports, universities and football stadiums. They are not doing all this under the auspices of a development aid programme, however. Chinese firms under state direction are obtaining from Africa raw materials that they badly need for their home industries, such as metal ores, metals, oil and gas, as well as large areas of farmland. They are operating pragmatically and efficiently – and with very little concern for sustainability, environmental protection or industrial safety. Above all, though, and in marked contrast with the West, they do not link their investments to any political demands. Thus, Angola sought and obtained from China $1 billion in credit after the World Bank had refused to extend this sum to the country because of its endemic corruption. Chinese companies are building roads, railway lines and a telecommunications network in Angola. The credit from Beijing is being amortised through the supply of oil to China.

Many African politicians are grateful for this pragmatic Chinese approach. Treaty negotiations with the World Bank that could have lasted for five years or more before agreement was reached were concluded within three months by the Chinese, Senegal's former president Abdoulaye Wade told the *Financial Times*.[78] By taking this line, China has been extremely successful. In July 2016, Chinese foreign minister Wang Yi announced that, in the first six months of that year, agreements had been signed securing a further $46 billion of Chinese direct investments and commercial credit.[79]

Brazil, Russia, and India – the other BRIC countries – have also discovered the investment opportunities in Africa for themselves, as have Turkey and a number of Arab states. By comparison, Africa's once-dominant European trading partners, primarily Great Britain and France, have fallen badly behind. Even Germany, Europe's largest economy, only registers as an also-ran in Africa. In 2014, German direct investments in Africa amounted to €9.6 billion – less than in 2010. In that same year, only 810 German firms had direct investments on the continent.[80] 'Europe has lost its crown as the most important investor in Africa', commented the South African investment holding company Africa Investor.[81] As a result, many of the new huge infrastructure projects currently under way on the African continent are being undertaken with the cooperation of new partners. These include deepwater ports in Cameroon and Guinea-Bissau, the Benguela Railway in Angola, the oil pipeline from Chad to the Atlantic, dams in Sudan and Ethiopia, refineries in Nigeria, hydroelectric power stations in Uganda and Zambia, wind farms in Kenya and the continent's largest solar power installation, in South Africa.

Africa goes online

Likewise, the revolution in information and communications technology has not passed Africa by. Since 2010, the underwater fibre-optic cable system SEACOM has connected the south and east of Africa with Europe and Asia. Fully 75 per cent of the consortium that owns this system is in the hands of African investors. A total of 17,000 kilometres of underwater cable have been laid. For East Africa, which for a long time was reliant on expensive and slow satellite connections, the advent of fast broadband connectivity represents a great advance: it is now connected with the world and increasingly competitive as a result. The 'African lions' are not just on the move; they are also going online. Across Africa as a whole, the internet is spreading at breakneck speed, while at the same time the continent is the fastest-growing market in the world for mobile phones. In 2013, 720 million Africans already owned a mobile phone, and 67 million a smartphone. Some 167 million people regularly used the internet, and more than half of city dwellers in Africa were online. Plus, 52 million Africans were active on social media sites such as Facebook. Overall, the internet contributed $18 billion to the GDP of Africa. According to forecasts modelled by McKinsey, by 2025 there will be 360 million smartphones and 600 million internet users in Africa. The profits from e-commerce will total some $75 billion, while the internet's contribution to Africa's GDP will increase to $300 billion annually.[82]

Mobile technology is stimulating the microeconomy: farmers and fishermen can keep abreast of current market prices and adjust their warehousing and sales accordingly; haulage firms can react flexibly to fluctuations in supply and demand; tradesmen can be contacted while they are on the move. But the new communication possibilities are also being employed in lucrative emerging business fields. For instance, a recent success story is the banking service M-Pesa, which was developed by a Kenyan mobile phone company in conjunction with Vodafone. M-Pesa allows money transfers to be made via a smartphone without the user having to have their own bank account – a revolutionary idea in a country where only 15 per cent of the adult population has such an account. Deposits and withdrawals of cash are made through dedicated counters at petrol stations, supermarkets, kiosks and mobile phone shops. Launched in 2007, the system spread like wildfire throughout Kenya. By 2014, 68 per cent of the country's mobile phone owners were using M-Pesa, with a total cashflow via the service of over €900 million.[83] From there, M-Pesa went on to conquer other countries and regions. Across Africa, 18 million people now use it, and the money transfer service is also available to users in India and Afghanistan. In 2014, Romania became the first European country to introduce it, and since 2015 it has also been available in Albania. In the meantime, similar systems to M-Pesa have been successfully piloted in other African countries such as Nigeria, Gabon and Sudan.

Kenya is something of a pioneer in in the use of mobile phones as the basis for a whole series of services. One of the country's most successful internet enterprises is M-Kopa, which sells solar panels to small enterprises on a credit basis. These small modules can generate electricity in shops in the slums of Nairobi and in farmers' huts in the countryside, where there is no reliable mains electricity supply. Customers pay their instalments on a daily basis via their mobile, and once the payment has gone through, the solar panel is made available for use for the next 24 hours. Once the small businessmen have proved their creditworthiness and the solar kit has been paid off, they are also offered refrigerators, cooking pots, televisions or smartphones. 'Basically, we are a finance company,' says Nick Hughes, one of the founders of M-Kopa. 'We provide our customers with a bit of security and a credit facility.' Very successfully, as it turns out: to date, 325,000 solar kits have been sold, and 50,000 of them have already been fully paid for. Above all, the project benefits low-paid earners: 80 per cent of those taking credit live on less than $2 a day.[84]

In many places in Africa, new and innovative firms are springing up in the realm of e-commerce. For example, the Nigerian enterprise Jumia is engaged in setting up an African alternative to Amazon. It was founded in 2012 and has since spread to 11 African countries. International investors in Jumia include Goldman Sachs, the telecoms provider Orange and the Berlin firm Rocket Internet. Jumia is attempting to find intelligent ways of overcoming problems inherent in Africa and to adapt itself to local conditions. Unlike Amazon, its giant Seattle-based rival, Jumia doesn't supply its customers directly with goods it has itself imported, but works with local firms instead. They supply the goods on demand to the online store, and from there they are distributed to the customers. In this way, Jumia generally saves itself the time and expense of having to get customs clearance for the goods it sells – not to mention the necessary bribes that often go hand-in-hand with such transactions.[85]

These are just a few examples among many highly inventive business ideas in modern Africa. The continent has the world's greatest growth in the number of start-up businesses. Many young African entrepreneurs in the communications sector believe in the principle of leapfrogging – in other words, given that their home continent is still working its way towards greater prosperity, they rely on skipping over the resource-wasting technologies of Western industrial countries and proceeding with their own novel solutions.

The new middle class

Africa's economic surge may be gauged from various indicators: the new highways, the boom in private car ownership and the endless traffic jams in the ever-growing cities; the lavish bank headquarters and the business parks that are springing up in many places; the steadily rising cost of land for building and for farming in many cities; the flourishing luxury hotels, where no room costs under $300 a night; the modern shopping malls which cater to every consumer desire, provided one has a sufficiently well-stocked wallet to afford it; and the increasing number of internet users. The hopes of national and international employers in Africa rest particularly on the developing middle class, which is seen as the motor of progress. Even in 2010 McKinsey had already identified 15.7 million people as belonging to the African middle class – taking as its benchmark a daily income of at least $5$5. The African Development Bank (AfDB) has arrived at an even more optimistic assessment. It now counts some 350 million Africans – or a third of the total population – as middle class. On closer scrutiny, the basis for this remarkable finding becomes clear: for the AfDB, the African lower-middle class comprises even those who only earn between $2 and $4 a day, whereas the 'true' middle class is made up of those earning between $4 and $20 a day.[86] As Richard Dowden, former executive director of the Royal African Society, has trenchantly put it: 'I suppose if you count everyone who is lucky enough to eat every day as a "consumer" and you then call all consumers "middle class", then almost everyone can be counted.'[87] Yet even if the notion of a vast African middle class currently remains something of a mirage, the desire of young Africans to better themselves and live lives of prosperity can nevertheless be felt everywhere – along with the motivation to do what is necessary to effect that change. This may not happen as quickly as many economists would hope, but over the coming years, they will undoubtedly be able to identify an ever-growing number of 'self-confident citizens who are in employment, and who predominantly live in cities, buy houses, drive mid-range cars and invest in their children's education – just like middle-class citizens the world over.'[88]

Different stages of development

The financial advisors, bankers and institutions who solicit for investment in Africa are no strangers to superlatives. Not even the World Bank, which annually elects a 'reformed country of the year'. In recent years, two African countries have been awarded this accolade – Rwanda in 2010 and Morocco in 2012. Yet amidst all the optimism that financial institutions are predisposed to spread, it should not be forgotten that the 54 countries on the continent of Africa are at very different stages of development. On closer inspection, then, a more nuanced picture emerges. In 2015, a series of countries with high growth rates and relatively stable political situations – Ethiopia, Côte d'Ivoire, Kenya, Morocco and Rwanda – accounted for one-fifth of the total GDP for Africa. Their economies are proving to be increasingly competitive and their growth is not solely dependent on natural resources. Alongside them, another group of countries had combined earnings that made up 43 per cent of Africa's GDP. These states also show relatively high growth rates, but are not nearly as stable as the first group and, in addition, are heavily reliant upon raw materials and natural resources. This group includes include countries such as Angola, the Democratic Republic of Congo, Nigeria and Zambia. A third group comprises countries with low growth rates, such as South Africa and Madagascar, together with countries that experienced the Arab Spring – Egypt, Libya and Tunisia. This last group contributed some 38 per cent to the continent's GDP.

Behind the attractive façade, the reality frequently appears quite different. The situation of several countries formerly held up as beacons of hope for Africa now presents a rather sobering picture. After South Sudan gained its independence in 2011, growth rates of over 20 per cent were forecast for it. Today, a dreadful civil war is raging in the world's youngest country, and it is facing ruin. The list of the most fragile countries in the world, which is compiled every year by the Fund for Peace organisation, was headed in 2016 by four African states: Somalia, South Sudan, the Central African Republic and Sudan. Two other African countries, Chad and the Democratic Republic of Congo, were among the 10 countries said to be most in danger of collapse.[89] By many measures of development, such as rates of literacy or access to dentistry, Africa continues to bring up the rear. Two out of every three Africans still suffer from hunger, according to Greg Mills in his book *Why Africa is Poor*.[90] In some regions, the infrastructure is worse than at the end of the colonial era. And most states are still lacking good governance, transparency of power and legal security. To this day, hope and misery remain close bedfellows in Africa.

The African paradox: the example of Ethiopia

The African paradox can be seen in all its many facets in the country of my birth, Ethiopia. Ethiopia is widely regarded as the 'growth star' of Africa.[91] Since 2003, the Ethiopian economy has been growing at a rate of 8 to 10 per cent annually.[92] Many international businesses have found the country to be a cost-effective manufacturing location. Clothing companies like H&M and KiK now have their garments made in Ethiopia. In addition, producers of consumer goods such as Unilever or the drinks company Diageo have production facilities in the country. The capital Addis Ababa in particular is undergoing a boom period: office blocks and hotels are shooting up wherever you look, and the streets are crammed with SUVs and lorries. In the autumn of 2015, the first section of the city's light rail system came into operation, built and run by Chinese investors. After South Africa's Gautrain network, it is the first modern urban transport system to be constructed south of the Sahara. In 2016 a new stretch of overland railway was opened from Addis Ababa to the port of Djibouti, also thanks to Chinese support.

In the far west of the country, on the Blue Nile, the Ethiopian government has ordered construction of the Grand Ethiopian Renaissance Dam (GERD). By 2018, it will be built as the largest dam on the continent, generating three times as much hydroelectric power as the famous Aswan High Dam in Egypt. According to official figures, the country is investing $4.8 billion into the project, though the actual costs have been put still higher.[93] Yet by the summer of 2017, work on the project was only 60 per cent complete.[94] The dam is part of the current administration's plan to electrify the entire country within a decade and to make Ethiopia the largest energy producer in Africa – and to achieve all this principally through 'green' electricity from renewable resources such as hydro, wind, solar and geothermal energy. It is an ambitious project, to be sure: so far, barely a quarter of Ethiopian households are connected to the electricity grid. There is not even a reliable power supply in the capital, and blackouts are commonplace. It is more than questionable whether this gigantic prestige project will ever come into operation. Moreover, the plan has sparked huge international controversy: Egypt is fearful that the dam will siphon off fully two-thirds of the Nile's water – thus depriving the country of its fertile Nile mud – and has protested vehemently against its construction. No doubt largely as a result of this, international investors are giving GERD a wide berth.

Ethiopia also has to contend with other adversities. In 2015, the two annual rainy seasons almost completely failed to materialise. Most of the country's dams that had already been built produced no electricity because the river levels were too low. The drought conditions have persisted ever since; the Blue Nile

Haus Publishing 65253 African Exodus

has dwindled to a trickle. Many experts now doubt whether the huge lake to be created by the new dam will ever fill to capacity. Worse still, a lack of rainfall meant that in 2015 and 2016 Ethiopia faced widespread famine – the country's worst for 30 years. The drought caused seeds to wither and die in the fields, and there was no grass for cattle, goats and sheep to graze on. Livestock died in their hundreds of thousands. This presented an existential threat to the nomadic peoples inhabiting the north of the country, who live off the meat and milk of their herd animals. Crop failures triggered huge hikes in the price of food. Around 18 million people, almost one-fifth of the country's population, have in the interim been forced to rely upon food supplies from abroad.[95]

This situation has not only hit Ethiopia's rural population. The inhabitants of the supposedly booming capital have also felt its effects. The last time I visited my homeland, I noticed on the central market place in Addis Abeba – which is called the 'Mercato' – a collection of huts. Their occupants were offering *gursha* (an Amharic word best translated as 'morsels'). Originally, this was a special gesture of hospitality; whenever one receives guests in Ethiopia, the age-old tradition has been to prepare them a celebratory meal. In the course of this, the host offers the guest a piece of injera – the traditional flatbread that is made from a cereal known as teff and is considered the national dish of Ethiopia – and places it into his or her open mouth as a welcoming gesture. Over time, however, this ritual has taken on a different meaning. The huts on the market square contained a wall with a slot set in it, covered by a flap; beneath the slot was a pile of sandbags. Outside the first hut I spotted, a large crowd of people – perhaps as many as 300 – were standing in line. (Actually, it would be more accurate to say that many of those waiting were squatting on the ground.) I went up to one of them and asked him: 'What's up with you? Are you ill?' He replied: 'No, but I haven't eaten anything in three days.' All of them were waiting to be admitted. When they got to the hut, they knelt on the sandbags so that their mouth was on a level with the slot in the wall. A voice asked 'For 25 cents or a birr [the principal Ethiopian unit of currency]?' Most people responded 'For a birr.' After paying, the kneeling person opened their mouth, and a morsel of food was pushed through the slot. The recipient then stood up, left the hut and the next person came in. For most of those standing in line, this was the only meal that they would eat that day. Today, tens of thousands of people in the capital of Ethiopia are subsisting on this daily morsel.

The example of Ethiopia demonstrates clearly that the growth figures many African countries are so fond of citing actually tell us very little. They start from a very low base, and any economic upturn passes by the vast majority of the populace in any case. Yet the yardstick for judging the development of African countries cannot simply be whether a limited number of people gain access to the living standard of the wealthy elites. Instead, we should be asking the question: 'What has been the effect on the purchasing power of ordinary Africans? And how has the life of a simple African farmer changed in the last 40 years?' The outcome in this context is sobering in comparison with most developing nations in Asia. A Chinese peasant can justifiably claim: 'Once I had a petrol lamp, now I've got mains electricity. Once I had to till my land with a team of oxen, now I can go to the farm collective and borrow a tractor. Before, I only had rice and beans to eat, but now I can afford to eat meat once or twice a week. Before I didn't have a clue about the written word, now I can read and write.' What can an African farmer say about himself, though? Over centuries, his situation has barely changed.

220 million Africans are starving

'Food security is a basic human right,' ran a declaration issued by the European Parliament. 'It is achieved when all people, at all times, have physical and economic access to suitable, safe and nutritious food to meet their dietary needs and preferences for an active and healthy life.'[96] Yet, even at the beginning of the twenty-first century, there are millions of people in the world who are being denied this fundamental human right. According to statistics from the Food and Agriculture Organization of the UN (FAO), in 2016 there were some 815 million people worldwide suffering starvation or malnourishment; that figure corresponded to 11 per cent of the global population.[97] Over half of those starving lived in Asia and almost one-third on the continent of Africa. Although the number of malnourished around the world had fallen by 167 million over the past 10 years, the development targets set at the World Food Summit in 1996 were still far from being achieved. At that conference, 182 countries had committed themselves to halving the number of starving people in the world by 2015. And while the number of malnourished people had clearly declined in South and East Asia, the picture in sub-Saharan Africa was very different: there, a total of 206 million people were suffering from starvation in 2005, and by 2015 that figure had risen to 220 million. Taken across the continent as a whole, the proportion of starving among the population at large was 25 per cent. All advances in combatting hunger had been undone in particular by the rapid population growth.

The annual Global Hunger Index (GHI) prepared by the International Food Policy Research Institute presents a more complex picture. The GHI calculations factor in a number of different indicators – for example, the proportion of children displaying signs of malnutrition and growth retardation, along with the mortality rate. Here, too, an improvement in the fight against malnutrition is apparent. Thus, the global GHI decreased from 35.4 points in 1990 to 21.7 points in 2017.[98] In Africa, too, the rates of starvation also declined according to this index, though sub-Saharan Africa, at 32.2 points, still had one of the highest factors of anywhere in the world. According to estimates by the World Bank, 45 to 50 per cent of Africa's entire population south of the Sahara were living below the poverty line, making the region the poorest in the world.

Most people who are starving do not die directly of hunger. They succumb to infections and diseases to which their under-nourished bodies can no longer put up resistance.[99] Yet how can it be that, according to expert testimony, the agricultural sector worldwide has the capacity to feed 12 billion people – in other words, five billion more than currently exist on Earth – and still 330 million Africans are starving? I know of many Africans, in Ethiopia and elsewhere, who regard starvation as a fate that has been ordained by God. However, the causes of starvation are unequivocally the work of man, as in the case of the famine of 2011–12 in Somalia – to date the worst this century, causing some 258,000 people to perish, according to UN studies. In that country, which decades of civil war had left without any effective state authority, international aid organ-isations found it virtually impossible to reach people in need. Yet not only local warlords but also US forces operating in the region blocked consignments of aid from getting through. The US saw such deliveries as support for the Islamist al-Shabaab militia, which they were targeting in their War on Terror.[100]

Meteorologists held the climatic phenomenon known as El Niño – which disrupts global weather patterns every five to seven years – largely responsible for the famine that struck Ethiopia in 2015–16. Other countries on the continent have also been affected by the prolonged drought: in East Africa, Ethiopia's neighbours Djibouti, Eritrea, Somalia and Sudan; in the south Angola, Zambia, Malawi, Mozambique, Namibia, Zimbabwe and Botswana, plus part of South Africa as well. Yet El Niño is a regular and recurrent event. Preparations should have been made to combat it. On previous occasions when this climatic phenomenon hit, emergency stores of grain were laid in well in advance.

The reasons for starvation are of a different, structural nature. In Ethiopia, for example, 80 per cent of people still earn their livelihood from farming. The great majority of farmers till their fields in exactly the same way as in biblical times, with a pickaxe or with wooden ploughs drawn by teams of oxen. They cannot afford agricultural machinery. There is a lack of high-quality seed, fertilisers and irrigation systems. The farmers practise subsistence farming; in other words, they produce no more than they require to feed themselves and their families. Agricultural productivity in Ethiopia is only half that of neighbouring Kenya. And even if they had the necessary means, Ethiopian farmers have absolutely no incentive to invest since the land that they cultivate does not belong to them. It is state property, as dictated by the Marxist ideology of the ruling party the Ethiopian People's Revolutionary Democratic Front (EPRFD), which governs the country with an iron fist. At the same time, Ethiopia has sold or leased an area of land equivalent to the size of Belgium to Saudi Arabian, Indian and Chinese agribusinesses – and while hunger stalks the land, Ethiopia is busy exporting wheat in order to obtain foreign currency.

Land-grabbing

It is not only in Ethiopia but also in many other countries south of the Sahara that most farmers practise subsistence farming. Over 90 per cent of the poorest people in sub-Saharan Africa derive their income from agriculture, and overall agricultural productivity there is lower than in any other region of the world.[101] In these circumstances, so-called land-grabbing has become a serious problem for the whole of Africa. The perpetrators are both private and state investors but also large agricultural concerns, who either buy up farmland or lease it on a long-term basis in order to use it for the production of basic commodities for their domestic markets. Financial markets and multinationals alike have discovered that land represents a lucrative investment. Borrowing from the language of investment banking, they use the term 'land banks' to denote profitable farmland. The acquisition of land is an investment 'like gold, only better', declared Chris Mayer, a finance expert for the US investment consultancy Stansberry Research, in 2009.[102]

The scale of land purchases around the world has been immense, occurring in South America and Southeast Asia as well as on the continent of Africa. Ownership of at least 5 per cent of all the farmland in Africa has changed hands over the past few years, while, at the time of writing, negotiations are ongoing regarding a further 20 to 30 per cent of available land. In November 2017, the independent online database Land Matrix put the total scope of land-grabbing deals worldwide at 48.9 million hectares. That figure took into account purchases that had actually been concluded as well as those that were still in the pipeline. With 17.25 million hectares, Africa represented a prime investment target for international speculators.[103]

Among the African countries most affected by this speculation are precisely those with a high proportion of starving people, such as South Sudan and Sudan, the Democratic Republic of Congo, Ethiopia, Mozambique, Tanzania and Sierra Leone. The most significant investors in land come from countries like China, India, Malaysia and Indonesia – countries which themselves can barely provide enough land for their rapidly expanding populations to farm. In the Democratic Republic of Congo alone, China is said to have leased more than 2.8 million hectares of land in order to cultivate the largest palm oil plantation in the world.[104] Similarly, the Gulf states, in which desert conditions make farming nigh on impossible, are acquiring large tracts of land on the continent of Africa. Even African states themselves are getting in on the act: in the fertile Niger Delta in Mali, for example, Libya took out a 50-year lease on 250,000 hectares of land for the cultivation of rice. The subsistence farmers displaced by this deal were forcibly relocated to areas lacking a reliable water supply. This transaction was engineered by the former Libyan dictator Colonel Muammar Gaddafi, and like most such deals it was negotiated behind closed doors.

The proponents of the large-scale global acquisition of land see in it the potential for a rational exploitation of farmland that has hitherto been either unused or underused. They maintain that land-grabbing is an indispensable tool in the fight against world hunger – but the truth looks very different in practice. The indigenous population derive almost no benefit from these acquisitions of land. Just 8 per cent of the land acquired in this way in Africa is currently being used for the cultivation of food crops. Some 44 per cent of the land is exploited for other purposes, while a further 12 per cent has been turned over to 'flex crops', which – depending on market demand – can be processed into biofuel, animal feed or human foodstuffs.[105] In particular, global biofuel refineries have staked a claim to a large proportion of the land. Mindful of the dwindling deposits of crude oil, these fields are now being touted as the 'oilfields of the future' and Africa has become a kind of 'diesel refinery' for industrialised nations, primarily those in Europe.[106] Even in locations where foodstuffs are being grown, the local population is not profiting from it. The crops that have been planted are almost exclusively destined for export. Small-scale farmers, herders, fishermen, farm labourers and nomadic peoples are the ones to suffer. Land that is sold or leased to foreign investors can no longer be used to grow food for local communities. People thereby lose their access to land and water, facilities that are vital for their survival.

The rose plantations of Ethiopia have become a *cause célèbre* in this regard. In Gambela, the country's most fertile region, hundreds of thousands of hectares of prime agricultural land are being used by foreign concerns to grow flowers. The original inhabitants of the region, the Anuak, who number about 500,000, were driven from their smallholdings to make way for the plantations.[107] In the meantime, Ethiopia has become the largest exporter of cut flowers in the world after Kenya. In 2014, the country exported flowers to the value of $250 million. On the farms around Addis Ababa alone, 2.5 billion roses are cut annually and stored in climate-controlled warehouses before being airfreighted to Europe.[108] Almost no labour law constraints are placed on the international producers of these goods – which are primarily from India, China, South Korea and the Arabian Peninsula. Children under the age of 10 are employed in the greenhouses, working eight-hour days for the equivalent of €1 or even less.

This same scene is replicated almost everywhere in Africa: if they create any jobs at all on the land they have leased, the big farming concerns only create poorly paid ones with substandard working conditions. In addition, the intensive cultivation methods they employ do environmental damage – through increased water usage, the clear-felling of woodland or just general overuse of the soil. Worse still, the companies in question deliberately seek out countries with poor governance and weak state agencies as sites for their business. In so doing, they profit from vague land ownership conditions and take possession of smallholdings that have been cultivated for centuries on the basis of customary rights of usage. Alternatively, they claim that the fields they have set their sights on are unsuitable for arable farming – yet apparently perfectly suitable for growing jatropha, the raw plant material for the manufacture of biodiesel. Small farmers are mostly helpless in the face of this onslaught by large agribusiness concerns, which work hand in hand with the countries' governments and local authorities. These agencies often put the land at the investors' disposal for a pittance. The going rate in Africa for an area the size of a football pitch is around €5 to €10, whereas the cost of leasing a comparable tract of land in Europe would be €400 or more. Not infrequently, the sums paid do not even go into public accounts but disappear into private individuals' pockets. Corruption is endemic. 'In most African countries,' writes Lorenzo Cotula, a principal researcher at the International Institute for Environment and Development, in his comprehensive study of land-grabbing in Africa, 'land is mainly used as a vehicle for extracting value [...] In this context, attracting foreign capital provides national elites with opportunities for business activities, political patronage and personal gain.'[109]

While their own populations go hungry, the ruling elites of Africa's poorest states are busy selling off their land to foreign enterprises. It is not uncommon for local farmers – as in Mali and Ethiopia – to be violently driven from their lands.

Land-grabbing has destroyed people's lives and uprooted families, made whole areas destitute and undermined the stability of entire regions. Price increases for foodstuffs on the global market have further accelerated the process of land-grabbing and driven up the cost of agricultural land steeply in both emerging economies and industrialised nations. This has made cheaper land in developing countries even more attractive to investors. Likewise, the transformation of arable land into fields for growing biofuels further stokes the competition for land. The upshot of this is that 23 per cent of all farmland in Sudan is in foreign hands, while in Mozambique it is 28 per cent, and in Sierra Leone 40 per cent; the figure is even as high as 85 per cent in Gabon.[110] Banks rocked by the financial crisis have found in land banks a lucrative new form of investment, promising annual rates of return of 20 per cent or more. Data compiled by the Land Matrix shows that US investors are by far the most active, acquiring almost 6 million hectares through purchase or lease, much of it in Africa, from 2000 to 2016; the UK was the fifth-largest investor, with around 2 million hectares.[111]

In October 2012, the president of the FAO, José Graziano da Silva, compared land-grabbing in Africa to conditions in the nineteenth-century Wild West, and called for a 'sheriff' to restore law and order.[112] The people of Africa have been waiting in vain for this sheriff to ride into town ever since. The UN felt that it was enough simply to issue voluntary guidelines on 'the responsible governance of tenure of land, fisheries and forests in the context of national food security' – a collection of resolutions and well-meaning precepts. This document states that access to land is an integral element of human rights and that existing claims to land ownership and people's access to natural resources should be respected. Those directly affected by land-grabbing should be listened to and involved in agreements. The FAO guidelines advocate the peaceful resolution of conflicts and call for public bodies and private concerns alike to take a responsible attitude to social and economic sustainability.[113] Yet they do not provide for any sanctions against companies that infringe these guidelines – or against governments that promote exploitative land acquisition in their countries and benefit financially from such arrangements.

Africa's test: the population explosion

Surely the greatest test for Africa will be whether and how it can begin to rein in its rapid growth in population. There are currently around 7.54 billion people on Earth, and every minute this figure increases by 159. According to forecasts by the German Foundation for World Population, the global population will have grown to 8.6 billion by 2030 and 9.8 billion by 2050.[114] In its latest estimate of population, the UN projected that the number of people on Earth will have reached 11.2 billion by 2100. The most rapid growth in population is taking place primarily in Asia and Africa. In mid-2017, there were some 1.25 billion people living in Africa. By 2030 this number will likely climb to 1.71 billion and by 2050 to 2.57 billion. The most dramatic increase is in countries south of the Sahara. By 2050 this region, with an estimated population in that year of almost 2.2 billion, will be home to double the number of people currently living there (estimated as 1 billion in 2017). Worldwide, over the past 50 years, the average number of children a woman gives birth to has halved from 5 to 2.5. By contrast, in sub-Saharan Africa the number has decreased much more slowly over the same period, from 6.6 to 5.

Several factors have been held responsible for this unchecked growth in population. For one thing there is the young age distribution on the African continent. Over half of all Africans are now below 25 years of age, with around 40 per cent aged less than 15. In 2015, the three nations with the youngest age profiles were all in Africa: the average age in Mali was 16.1, in Uganda 15.6 and in Niger just 15.2.[115] All these young people still have their child-bearing years ahead of them. Another factor is the large number of unwanted births. There is a serious lack of sex education and advice, and above all of access to contraceptives. While around 70 per cent of married women in Europe use contraceptives of one kind or another, in sub-Saharan Africa that figure drops dramatically to only 30 per cent.[116] Many African women deliberately choose to have lots of children. They regard large families as the best form of social security, in the absence of provision by the state for care in old age. If one or two of those many children survive, the theory goes, then they will be able to look after their parents in later life.

This is not a specifically African problem. Well into the nineteenth century, large families were also the norm in Europe. A peasant woman in the Middle Ages bore on average five to six children, while in the Early Modern period it was not uncommon for a woman to give birth as many as 20 times over the course of her marriage. A large number of the offspring would die before reaching adulthood, often soon after their birth. Squalor, lack of hygiene, epidemics, hunger and wars all contributed to this high rate of infant mortality. But the example of Europe demonstrates that, with growing economic development, better health provision and social welfare, the birth rate on the African continent could also be permanently reduced.

However, quick solutions to this problem are nowhere in sight. In 1970 Ethiopia had a population of 25 million, whereas today it is 105 million, making it the continent's most populous country after Nigeria. Its population is estimated to reach 165 million by 2050. The growth of cities has been especially dramatic: In 1970 Addis Ababa had just 600,000 inhabitants, while today 7 million people live there. The most densely populated city in the whole of Africa is Lagos in Nigeria, which has grown from 37,000 inhabitants at the start of the twentieth century to over 15 million in the early twenty-first. Since no one can say exactly how many people are living there, this figure may already have reached 20 million. In the 1970s – when, as a result of its rapidly expanding population, Lagos was faced with collapse – a new Nigerian capital was founded at Abuja. However, this did nothing to change the chaotic situation in Lagos. Quite the opposite, in fact: the city continues to act as a magnet for the country's poor, who flood there in hope of finding work. In the vast slums of Ajegunle and Amukoko, there is no functioning infrastructure and no running mains water or electricity. It is beyond the reach of the municipal authorities, and public order is maintained there by gangs of young petty criminals, the so-called Area Boys. These shanty towns, with their mountains of refuse and open drains and sewers, form ideal breeding grounds for mosquitoes. Little wonder that malaria is on the increase there.

The questions remain: how will Africa manage to feed all these people? What future can it offer its millions of young people, with all their aspirations and potential? How can it provide them with schools and other educational institutions and a functioning healthcare system? And what can be done to ensure that this huge population earns a proper livelihood?

Climate change and destabilisation

All the while, the threat of climate change is only deepening existing inequalities. In comparison with the period before industrialisation, the average global temperature has already risen by 0.9 degrees Celsius. The effects of climate change have already been felt across the Southern Hemisphere in the form of droughts, water shortages, hurricanes and erratic monsoon rains. The desert is expanding throughout the Sahel region. And this is just the beginning. The Intergovernmental Panel on Climate Change (IPCC) points in its fifth assessment report to the global dangers of this phenomenon: 'Since average temperatures around the globe by 2050 will rise by an estimated 2 to 4 degrees, there will – if all other conditions stay the same – be a potential in future for great changes in global patterns of interpersonal violence, intercommunal conflict and social instability.'[117]

Particularly in Africa, climate change threatens to fuel existing conflicts.[118] In his 2008 book *Climate Wars*, the Canadian journalist Gwynne Dyer paints an apocalyptic picture of a world affected by accelerating climate change. In Dyer's view, the wars of the future will be sparked by climate. He predicts a huge increase in the number of refugees from the Southern Hemisphere, people who have been starved out by drought or forced to leave their homes by rising sea levels and are trying to make it to the North; on the other side are those countries that can still produce enough food because they are located at higher latitudes, and which fight tooth and nail to keep out the tide of refugees who are demanding their share.[119] It need not come to this if the international community resolves to take drastic measures against global warming. Yet it is also the case that, however great an effort we make now, we can no longer do anything to influence the temperature pattern over the next 20 to 30 years.

The destabilising effect of climate change can already be felt in various regions of Africa, for instance in Sudan and northern Nigeria. There, soil degradation has forced thousands of farmers and livestock herders to leave their villages. This has been a contributory factor in the spread of the Islamist terrorist militia Boko Haram throughout the north of Nigeria. Similarly, rises in the price of wheat and the resultant tripling of the cost of bread in Egypt helped fuel protests against the regime of President Hosni Mubarak during the Arab Spring of 2010.

Africa's greatest burden: corrupt regimes and elites

Africa is poor: this statement still holds true in 2018. Wars and other armed conflicts, diseases like AIDS and malaria, land-grabbing and climate change are the heavy burdens weighing down on the continent. But Africa is not poor because people there don't want to work hard. One of the main reasons for Africa's poverty is its governments and its elites. These have become the greatest imposition on Africa. Many of its rulers follow the example of the West and parade their wealth for all to see. They have no concern for the best interests of their people. The political elites in most African countries profit from the status quo and are not interested in effecting change.

This is clearly in evidence in those countries that are particularly well endowed with mineral resources and oil – Nigeria, for example. The largest oilfields in the whole of Africa were discovered in the 1950s in the Niger Delta. Foreign oil companies built enormous drilling installations and before long petrodollars in their millions were flowing into Nigeria. The giant petroleum multinationals had no concern for environmental protection or the welfare of local communities. Over the last 40 years, Nigeria has earned more than $400 billion from its oil exports – in 2000, this income amounted to $325 for every man, woman and child in the country. Yet, over that same period, the proportion of Nigerians living on less than $1 a day grew from 19 to 90 million.[120] To this day, the oil business continues to play a crucial role in Nigeria's economy. And to date the average per-capita income in Nigeria remains below that of most other African countries.

Nigeria: the curse of resources

The Nigerian elite grew rich on the income from oil exports – which soon exceeded the tax revenues raised within the country – and lived in the lap of luxury on the proceeds. They lost little sleep over the plight of their fellow Nigerians. In this way Nigeria was transformed into a kleptocracy, and Nigerian corruption soon became legendary. No one can say exactly how many billions of oil revenue have flowed illegally into the pockets of the elite and their offshore accounts. In 2007, Nigeria's anti-corruption commissioner gave his appraisal that between 1960 and 1999, a total of $300 billion had been embezzled.[121] Nobody was called to account for this misappropriation of state funds. The American journalist Karl Maier pulled no punches in describing the situation in Nigeria in 1999 in his book *This House Has Fallen*: 'Nigerians live in a criminally mismanaged corporation where the bosses are armed and have barricaded themselves inside the company safe.'[122]

The ruling elites allowed some funds to trickle down in exchange for political support. In this way, corruption spread to all levels of Nigerian society and also heightened ethnic and religious tensions. Before long, no one wanted to or could rely any longer on state institutions. Social cohesion evaporated, creating a vacuum at the heart of the country. This paved the way for fundamentalist ideologies such as that peddled by Boko Haram, which declared war on all Western interests. The vast majority of people in the Muslim north of Nigeria may well be horrified by the brutality of this Islamist terror group, yet, insofar as they feel they have been systematically disadvantaged for decades by the Christian-dominated south of the country, a significant minority in the north regard the militants as an 'institution' that might be in a position to counterbalance the corrupt government.

Under the presidency of Olusegun Obasanjo, Nigeria took steps in the first decade of the twenty-first century to try and stem the tide of corruption. Obasanjo called corruption 'the greatest challenge facing Nigeria' and, in collaboration with Transparency International, he launched an anti-corruption campaign. This initiative was designed to bring greater transparency to the oil exploration sector and enable Nigerian citizens to 'call their government to account'. Since its inception, some things have certainly changed. Human rights organisations have set their sights on the business practices of global concerns working in Nigeria – and firms listed on international stock exchanges fear nothing so much as damning headlines. Likewise, President Muhammadu Buhari, a Muslim from the north of the country who was elected in May 2015, has also declared war on corruption. Even so, the fight against the system of privilege and patronage is an arduous and long one. It will be difficult tackling the notorious 'curse of resources' – the deeply corrosive effect that Nigeria's mineral wealth has had on its body politic and system of government.

At the time of writing, Nigeria is once again experiencing the negative consequences of its dependency on oil. Some 40 per cent of the country's GDP is derived from this sector, together with around 80 per cent of state revenues. Numerous infrastructure projects are supported by money from the oil industry, too. But the current dramatic slump in the price of oil worldwide has placed many of these projects in doubt, for Nigeria's bloated state bureaucracy alone swallows up around 90 per cent of the budget.[123] In order to balance the books, Nigeria would need oil to be priced at $110 a barrel; in autumn 2017, the price on the Rotterdam spot market and other key international markets was just $55 a barrel. There is nothing to indicate that the price of oil will rise significantly in the foreseeable future.

The Katanga boom

The curse of resources has also affected other African countries and regions that are rich in minerals. Take, for example, Katanga in the south of the Democratic Republic of Congo, by far the country's wealthiest province. Some 34 per cent of the world's cobalt deposits and around 10 per cent of its copper reserves are found here. Under Mobutu, these ores were extracted by the state monopoly mining concern Gécamines, which had been established during the era of Belgian colonialism. Joseph Kabila, who came to power in 2001, cleared the way for the privatisation of mining operations in the Democratic Republic of Congo. Investors appeared in droves and the sell-off of the country's mineral wealth began. In many cases, foreign concerns were granted dream concessions. An investigative commission appointed by the government later determined that the estimated price of the deposits had been systematically undervalued. Moreover, regulations designed to protect miners' working conditions and the environment were ignored and excavation areas were expanded without official authorisation. Rather than the much-trumpeted supposed $200 million in tax revenue from the mining operations, just $27 million flowed into the state coffers – little wonder, given that the companies in question were guaranteed tax exemptions for up to 30 years.[124] This economic boom also exacerbated social tensions within the country. The hordes of freelance prospectors that had formerly excavated the ores with primitive tools were ousted from the region. The governor of Katanga accused the central government of withholding the share of tax and customs revenues that it was due. And the ordinary people of Katanga benefitted hardly at all from the mining boom.

The spectacular so-called 'deal of the century' that the Congolese government concluded with the People's Republic of China in September 2007 has so far done little to alleviate the situation. This contract granted China the right to mine 10 million tons of copper and 600,000 tons of cobalt in Katanga. In exchange, China agreed to invest $3 billion in restoring the mining infrastructure of the region and a further $6 billion in a huge reconstruction programme. This included building 3,500 kilometres of asphalted roads, and the construction of 176 clinics and hospitals as well as airports and two universities.[125] Despite this, to date, tarmac roads, schools and hospitals are a rarity outside of the provincial capital Lubumbashi. As a result, discontent has been rising among local people, and calls for the province to secede from the Congo have been growing louder. The rebel militia Mai Mai Kata Katanga (Swahili for 'Break Away, Katanga') has in the meantime begun an armed insurrection, stopping at nothing in pursuit of its aims. Entire villages have been razed to the ground and their inhabitants butchered and raped. According to figures from the UNHCR, 400,000 Katangans have already been displaced by the violence and sought shelter in refugee camps.[126]

Kiki the Oil Magnate

The economy of the Republic of Congo, the small Western neighbour of the Democratic Republic of Congo, also relies primarily on oil. In 2015, it produced 290,000 barrels of crude. For the past 37 years – with a break of five years – the country has been governed by President Denis Sassou Nguesso. In the autumn of 2015, in the face of violent public protests, he held a referendum on a change to the constitution that would enable him to stand again for office in the elections due to be held in March 2016. The opposition boycotted the referendum. The day of the election was marred by assaults against opposition supporters by police officers using tear-gas. The mobile phone network was switched off, supposedly for reasons of security and public order, access to the Internet was blocked and a ban was imposed on the driving of all motor vehicles within the capital, Brazzaville.[127] Accusations that the poll had been rigged came from both within the country and abroad. Despite this, the country's electoral commission certified that Sassou Nguesso had been re-elected president, with 60 per cent of the votes cast. His son Denis Christel Sassou Nguesso, a member of parliament and member of the politburo of the ruling Congolese Workers Party, has been given the nickname 'Kiki the Oil Magnate'. He is general administrator of the state-owned oil company SNPC. Some years ago, reports began to circulate about his extended shopping trips to Paris, Dubai and Marbella. The president's family owns a number of luxury properties in France. Accusations have long been voiced that those belonging to the clique around Sassou Nguesso have amassed personal fortunes from the lucrative oil business. In the spring of 2016, Sassou Nguesso's name cropped up in the notorious Panama Papers: these documents suggest that as far back as the 1990s the Panamanian law firm Mossack Fonseca had set up an offshore shell company, based on the British Virgin Islands, for the president of the Republic of Congo.[128]

A system based on greed and bribery

The Panama Papers contained the names of a host of leading representatives of international firms doing lucrative business in Africa, alongside those of influential Africans such as: Bukola Saraki, the president of the Nigerian senate; Mounir Majidi, the personal secretary to the King of Morocco; Ian Kirby, the president of Botswana's Court of Appeal; and Kalpana Rawal, the acting president of Kenya's Supreme Court. Family members of former or current African heads of state – such as Clive Khulubuse Zuma, a nephew of South African president Jacob Zuma, for example – also appear in the papers.[129]

All of these individuals now need to explain themselves, for the great majority of Mossack Fonseca's clients made use of the firm's services for the purposes of tax evasion, the depositing of bribes or the concealment from the authorities of profits from deals involving oil or other raw materials.[130] The Panama Papers throw some light into the murky depths of a system of greed and bribery which to this day remains the norm in many African countries. Cautious estimates assume that, year on year, some €50 billion are still being siphoned off from Africa in the form of illegal money flows. These funds, which are shifted by means of corruption, money laundering and tax evasion, far exceed the sums that Africa receives every year in overseas development aid.[131] The involvement of African politicians in the Panama Papers furore, according to Lenny Kasoga, an economist at the University of Dar es Salaam in Tanzania, is 'a scandal for Africa and for governance in African countries'.[132]

On the global map of the Corruption Perceptions Index that

Transparency International publishes every year, the African continent appears, with depressing regularity, coloured uniformly in shades of red and dark red – indicating a high or very high degree of corruption, respectively. In the 2016 ranking accompanying the map, the most corrupt nations on Earth were Somalia and South Sudan, and of the 25 most corrupt countries, 14 were African. Alongside the two mentioned above, these were (in descending order): Sudan, Libya, Guinea-Bissau, Eritrea, Angola, the Republic of Congo, Chad, the Central African Republic, Burundi, the Democratic Republic of Congo, Zimbabwe and Uganda.[133]

The British-Sudanese entrepreneur and billionaire Mo Ibrahim, who campaigns for good governance in Africa, has since 2007 awarded a prize honouring exemplary former African heads of state, the Ibrahim Prize for Achievement in African Leadership. The prize money is among the most generous in the world: the winner receives a one-off payment of $5 million for the first 10 years and thereafter a yearly stipend for life of $200,000. In order to be eligible for the prize, the candidate must be a democratically elected African head of state who has stepped down from office within the previous three years and who during their time in office displayed exemplary governance. However, in its 10-year history, the prize has only been awarded four times – in the other years no candidate could be found who fulfilled the criteria. The last person to be so honoured was Hifikepunye Lucas Pohamba, in 2014, who had been the president of Namibia from 2005 to 2015.[134] The Ibrahim Foundation also runs an annual assessment of the quality of governance in Africa, named the Ibrahim Index. In 2016 the three top-ranking countries in this index were Mauritius, Botswana and Cape Verde. The worst-performing countries on the continent in terms of their governance were the Central African Republic, South Sudan and, in fifty-fourth and last place, the failed state of Somalia.[135]

Many governors and public servants in Africa still unashamedly subscribe to the system of personal enrichment. 'Of course I'm corrupt,' one high-ranking government official recently told me to my face, 'otherwise how could I feed my extended family of 40?' In many African countries, ministers of state earn a salary of less than €2,000 a month, and not infrequently they are expected to perform supplementary duties. 'Why did I make so-and-so a minister in the first place?' runs the thinking of some African heads of state. 'He ought to be making a living of his own.' In any event, I have never heard the phrase 'I am the first servant of my people' – as opposed to my clan – uttered in Africa.

The same standards that hold good for politicians the world over should also be applied to Africa's politicians; they should be paid a decent salary and furnished with a good official car. But taking payments for services rendered, either in kind or in the form of money, should be strictly forbidden – and infractions of this rule dealt with severely. It should always be borne in mind, though, that it takes two for corruption to flourish – the corruptor and the person who allows him- or herself to be corrupted. For a long time, European firms were all too keen to collude in bribery and corruption, and it is only recently that stricter compliance has come into force in Western boardrooms. It was not so very long ago that companies in many Western countries were able to write off the monies they used for bribes against tax.

Africa's so-called democracies

The African Development Bank advertises its services with the assertion that nowadays, with the exception of three countries, all the states of Africa have democratic constitutions. If only that were true! In most of these countries, democracy and good governance are actually not so very far advanced at all. At the regional World Economic Forum held in May 2016 in the Rwandan capital Kigali, the host country presented itself as being top of the class in the continent's democracy stakes. 'Rwanda is on the right track,' declared the economist and Africa expert Mike Cohen of the New York-based business information service Bloomberg. 'It is playing a leading role in curbing bureaucracy, guaranteeing tax incentives and improving governance. All these factors have helped Rwanda overcome its handicaps – such as the small size of the country, its lack of a port and its paucity of mineral resources.'[136] President Paul Kagame, who has been in office since 2000, has taken as his model the metropolis of Singapore; the intention is that one day the streets of Kigali will be as clean and safe as they are in the Far Eastern city-state. The president proudly points to his list of achievements: one-fifth of Rwanda's budget is being devoted to healthcare, while civil servants and many employees in the private sector also now have private health insurance. Some 90 per cent of all children attend primary school, with girls outnumbering boys in the classes. Among members of the Rwandan parliament, 64 per cent are women. Yet, in the would-be 'Switzerland of Africa', Kagame sits like an autocrat at the head of the ruling Rwandan Patriotic Front. At his last re-election in August 2010 he allegedly, according to figures issued by the national electoral commission, received 93 per cent of the total votes cast. But for all practical intents and purposes the opposition was excluded from taking part in the election, with the only 'opposition' candidates allowed to run being political allies of Kagame. The real opposition was cowed, while a number of politicians and journalists were assassinated.

Representatives of foreign NGOs were expelled from the country, all national NGOs were forced to toe the party line and the press was brought under state control.

A clause existed in the Rwandan constitution restricting the president's time in office to two periods of seven years each. On the basis of this stipulation, Kagame should have been disbarred from standing in the 2017 presidential race. But in December 2015 he organised a referendum proposing an amendment to the constitution that would allow him to remain in office after 2017. This plebiscite was held with just a week's notice. A legal objection to the referendum submitted by the only remaining independent opposition party, the Democratic Green Party of Rwanda, was dismissed within days.[137] According to official figures, over 98 per cent of the electorate approved the constitutional change; in the ensuing presidential election, held in August 2017, a similar overwhelming proportion allegedly supported Kagame's re-election for a third term.

Election results that read like those from the former Soviet Union have also been recorded in several other African countries. In October 2015, the president of Côte d'Ivoire Alassane Ouattara was confirmed in office in the first electoral round with over 83 per cent of votes. In Ethiopia, which calls itself a 'Federal Democratic Republic', prior to 2015 there was only a single opposition politician in parliament, with all the other seats being held by the ruling Ethiopian People's Revolutionary Democratic Front and its allies. In the last parliamentary elections in May 2015, the ruling party 'won' this final seat as well. No one in the world believes that things can possibly be above board in elections with these kinds of results. Prime Minister Hailemariam Desalegn, who took over this post in 2012 after the death of the long-serving premier Meles Zenawi, had pledged when he took office to relax the Ethiopian political system, but the opposite actually ensued. The government has taken as its template the Chinese system of state capitalism under the control of a single ruling party. Foreign observers have in the meantime taken to speaking in terms of a 'developing dictatorship'.[138] The opposition has been smashed, and all dissidents either have now left the country or are behind bars. Torture is the order of the day. There is no free press, the internet and social media are closely controlled and independent bloggers are hounded. In scarcely any other country in the world are there so many journalists in gaol. Peaceful demonstrations are put down by force of arms. The most recent brutal crackdown was on protests by the Oromo people who since the turn of 2015–16 had been campaigning against the expansion of the capital onto their fields and their imminent expulsion from their traditional homelands.[139] Over time, many students had also rallied to the Oromos' cause, and the protests spread to the Amhara region. By August 2016, they were already being spoken of as the 'most serious disturbances in the country for 25 years'.[140]

Another term in office or another coup

African constitutions are often not worth the paper they are written on. This is certainly the case in Burundi, Rwanda's neighbour and likewise a former Belgian colony. There, President Pierre Nkurunziza decided to simply ignore the constitution, which limited presidential terms in office. In April 2015 he announced that he would seek popular endorsement for a third term in the forthcoming elections. This prompted a constitutional crisis. Violent unrest erupted in various parts of the country. The vote was postponed on several occasions. When it finally took place in July 2015, voter participation in the capital Bujumbura was very small indeed, since most of the opposition parties boycotted the election. In spite of this, the country's electoral commission declared Nkurunziza the winner with 69 per cent of the vote. International observers determined that the vote had been neither free nor fair. Between April and December 2015, according to figures released by the UN high commissioner for human rights Zeid Ra'ad Al Hussein, 400 people were killed – most of them by Nkurunziza's police force and the Imbonerakure, the notorious militia of his party's youth wing, who were directed to sow terror in the streets of Bujumbura. Some 3,500 people were arrested and detained without any charges being brought against them, and more than 220,000 people fled to the neighbouring countries of Tanzania, Rwanda, and the Democratic Republic of Congo. There is nothing to suggest that the simmering conflict will be resolved any time soon. The UN has warned of a further destabilisation of the country and an impending civil war.[141]

Many modern African presidents attempt to cling on to power through illegal means. They refuse to acknowledge that their power is not boundless and that it has a time limit on it, preferring instead to regard their office as a hereditary post – indeed, as most of the founding fathers of postcolonial Africa before them who led their countries to independence also did. Thus Nkurunziza, who has close links to evangelical Christianity, called his presidency a 'God-given mandate'.[142] Many countries in Africa now find themselves faced with a dismal choice: another term in office for the incumbent, or another coup.[143]

Like the kings and princes of old, some of Africa's leaders today are even beginning to think in terms of dynasties. In three African states, the presidents have already managed to found just such a 'ruling house'. In Togo, after the death in 2005 of President Gnassingbé Eyadéma, who had ruled the country as an autocrat for almost 40 years, his son Faure Gnassingbé was installed as president by the Togolese army. He has been in power ever since and shows no sign of stepping down. In the Democratic Republic of Congo, after the assassination of Laurent Kabila in 2000, his son Joseph Kabila, who had previously held the post of commander-in-chief of the army, assumed the presidency; he 'inherited' a country torn apart by a long-running civil war. As his permitted two terms in office were drawing to a close, Joseph Kabila toyed with the idea of flouting the constitution and standing for re-election in November 2016. In the event, the country's electoral authority decided to postpone the election until at least April 2018; Kabila remains in power in the interim. In Gabon in 2009, Ali-Ben Bongo succeeded his father Omar Bongo, the de facto dictator of the country since 1967; Ali-Ben Bongo had been defence minister in his father's administration. Although the younger Bongo was elected president, Gabon does not have a democratic system of governance. Ali-Ben Bongo rules in the style of an absolutist monarch. The prisons of the capital Libreville are bursting at the seams and, despite its mineral wealth, the country is poverty stricken. Meanwhile, the president is reputed to be one of the richest men in Africa, and his family members have profited hugely from their proximity to the presidency. In France alone, the Bongo family is believed to own 39 properties, according to media sources in Gabon's neighbour Cameroon. The groundwork for Ali-Ben Bongo's lifetime presidency has already been laid thanks to his father, who in 2003 enacted the ubiquitous constitutional amendment lifting the restriction on the president's term of office.

People's patience runs out

There are strong indications that the ordinary people of Africa are no longer prepared to tolerate their rulers playing fast and loose with their constitutions. 'If constitutions are tailored like made-to-measure suits to individual presidents,' the Guinean writer Tierno Monénembo has said, 'entire countries will end up drifting into chaos.'[144]

Africa is beginning to rebel against its everlasting presidents and their despotic rule. – and not just in Burundi and the Republic of Congo. In Burkina Faso, for example, an attempt by the incumbent president Blaise Compaoré to change the constitution in 2014 failed. This amendment would have cleared the way for him to stand as president for a fifth term. Protests erupted against the plan throughout the country. Opposition leaders and trade unions called for a general strike. On 30 October 2014, the day of the planned referendum, the military seized power and declared that Blaise Compaoré had been ousted. But people continued with their demonstrations and succeeded in forcing the appointment of a civilian transitional president; free elections were scheduled. The people of Burkina Faso took to the streets once more in September 2015 when the Presidential Guard tried to stage a coup. The demonstrators were determined to defend democracy. In this they succeeded: the ballot of November 2015 saw 14 candidates stand for election. The chairman of the newly founded People's Movement for Progress (MPP), Roch Marc Kaboré, emerged victorious and was duly appointed president.

Friend or foe

Elections alone, however, are no guarantee of democracy. Africa can offer many tragic instances that bear out the truth of this assertion. Democracy does not just consist of elections with candidates representing a number of parties, but also of rules and control mechanisms, which those who have been elected must commit to observing. 'If there are no limits on the power of the winner, the election becomes a matter of life and death,' the British economist Paul Collier has written, in his 2010 book *War, Guns and Votes: Democracy in Dangerous Places*,[145] which deals with the question of democracy in the world's poorest countries. Being elected by a majority does not give a politician carte blanche to rule unchecked. Africa's potentates are well versed in the tried-and-tested strategies of manipulation that are employed throughout the world: scape-goating minorities, engaging in bribery on both a small and grand scale, eliminating opposition candidates and commit-ting electoral fraud. They have no conception of what political opposition means; they know of only friend or foe. There are more than 2,000 different languages in Africa, but not one of them contains an equivalent of the word 'opponent' as it is understood in Western democracies, from the cut-and-thrust of parliamentary debate between rival political parties. 'The supporter of another party may think differently from me, but I respect his opinion – and respect him as a person': this axio-matic dictum of democracy remains a mystery to most African leaders to this day. In precolonial times in Africa, the following sentence was frequently heard: 'Don't you know who I am? I am the enemy of so-and-so.' In other words, a person derived their social status from that of their sworn enemy. But Africa's modern autocratic rulers are harking back to even less enlight-ened times in their belief that any dissenting opinion must be crushed because it stands in the way of their self-advancement.

The value of institutions

If one interrogates the question of why democracy has such a hard time in Africa, another factor must be borne in mind: in many African countries, even today, there is an absence of a functioning state capable of furnishing its citizens with social peace, protection under the rule of law, working infrastructure and adequate educational and healthcare facilities. The institutions that guarantee good government are totally lacking – as is a system of separation of powers, which would rein in those rulers who refuse to obey the democratic rules of the game. In their comprehensive empirical study *Why Nations Fail*, the economists and political scientists Daron Acemoglu and James A. Robinson state that the proper functioning of state institutions is the decisive factor for the success or failure of a country. According to them, aspects like climate geography, language and culture only play a role insofar as they can influence the emergence of these institutions. If a state possesses 'inclusive' institutions like democratic elections, personal property rights and opportunities for economic advancement for the individual, its resources can be used to benefit everybody. The key thing, therefore, is to activate the talents, creativity and energies of the citizens of a country. A state that neglects large sectors of its populace can scarcely use its available potential – and hence is incapable of profiting in the long term from economic change.[146]

In many African countries, though, there is still nothing that warrants the name of a market economy; instead the 'subsistence economy' still predominates.[147] Substantial earnings do not derive from any entrepreneurial activity but simply from political control over lucrative resources. Those in power exact a high price for the allocation of concessions to exploit these resources – a system that opens the floodgates to corruption.

Profit is also realised from the indiscriminate taxation of foreign trade or the import of toxic waste or electronic scrap. Rulers also have to invest a considerable portion of their capital in safeguarding their hold on power – that is, in the military, police, secret service and loyal bureaucracies that help prop up this system. The fact is that such a system cannot be squared with democratic principles. Most of the population are left out in the cold. And as long as the elites keep profiting from it, as long as they can continue to safely salt away the income they derive from it, things will carry on just as they have always done – until the population finally loses patience with its rulers.

The failure of the African Union

But surely Africa has its own continent-wide umbrella organisation, an institution that must be in a position to bring about change? The African Union (AU), to which all African countries except Morocco belong, has set as its foremost objectives the strengthening of African unity and the fostering of solidarity between the peoples and nations of the continent. However, it has assiduously refrained from criticising individual African heads of state. Where good governance and democratisation are concerned, it would be wise not to set too much store by this organisation.

And yet at its inception the AU was intent on doing everything so much better than its predecessor, the Organisation of African Unity (OAU), which had served primarily as a stage on which African leaders could present themselves to the outside world and elevate their own importance. When the African heads of state met for their annual summit in Ethiopia's capital Addis Ababa in 1977, at the height of the Red Terror ravaging that country, they quite literally had to step over dead bodies in order to enter the Ethiopian parliament building. And yet, during the course of the summit, not a single African president spoke about the political situation in the host country. The tacit principle of non-interference in the internal affairs of individual states continued to hold sway. In the same way, the OAU turned a blind eye to the genocide in Rwanda and did nothing to intervene, just as it did when Somalia collapsed into a failed, lawless state. In contrast to this, the AU, which was founded in 2002, has made an express commitment to democratic principles, human rights and gender equality. Nevertheless, as before, the principle of non-intervention continues to shape the organisation's actions, as opposed to its rhetoric. Only in a few especially grave cases could the AU bring itself to temporarily suspend the memberships of individual states: for instance, Niger after the military coup in 2012, and the Central African Republic following the seizure of power there in 2013 by the Islamist rebel coalition Séléka. In both these cases, the suspension of membership only lasted for a few months or years at most. Egypt was temporarily suspended after the military coup of July 2013 that ousted the elected Muslim Brotherhood president Mohamed Morsi, yet it did not take long for the AU to rule that the regime of General Abdel Fattah el-Sisi had restored 'constitutional order' in Egypt and to welcome the country back into the fold – in spite of continuing human rights violations by the regime in Cairo. Since April 2016, there has been no African state that the AU has barred from its ranks.

In December 2015, though, a resolution of the AU Peace and Security Committee caused the world to sit up and take notice. It decided to dispatch a 5,000-strong peacekeeping force to Burundi, where President Nkurunziza's determination to cling on to power come what may had plunged the country into political crisis. The committee further resolved that, if Nkurunziza refused to assent to the mission, the troops should even be deployed against the will of the Burundian government. This would have marked a first in the history of the African Union. Yet the decision first needed to be ratified by the plenary session of the AU's heads of state and government, who met in Addis Ababa at the beginning of February 2016. However, the African heads of state lost no time in bringing the Peace and Security Committee to heel: no troops would be sent without the Burundian government's permission. But Nkurunziza set his face firmly against any such mission – as he also did against a resolution of the UN Security Council, which had proposed that an international police force should, at the behest of the UN, monitor Burundi's security situation and observance of human rights.

The African leaders continued to operate according to the principle of 'birds of a feather flock together'. This is also apparent in the attitude taken by African heads of state and government towards the International Criminal Court (ICC) in The Hague. Time and again, from Rwanda, Kenya, Uganda and many other African nations, the same accusations have been levelled at this tribunal, namely that it is 'anti-African' and 'neocolonial'. There have been repeated calls for Africa to withdraw en bloc from this body. Sudan's president Omar al-Bashir was given a warm welcome at the AU summit in the Rwandan capital Kigali in July 2016, despite the fact that he had for the past eight years been the subject of an international arrest warrant issued by the ICC. Although 34 African states are signatories to the ICC's founding Rome Statute, which obliges them to execute arrest warrants from the court, they have so far doggedly refused to allow al-Bashir to be extradited.

As of autumn 2017, more than 20 Africans – constituting the overwhelming majority of all those being sought – are on the ICC's list of indictees. In June 2016 Jean-Pierre Bemba, the former vice president of the Democratic Republic of Congo, was sentenced in The Hague to 18 years' imprisonment. He stood accused of orchestrating numerous war crimes and crimes against humanity, carried out by his rebel militia in 2002 and 2003 in the territory of the neighbouring Central African Republic. January 2016 saw the first former African head of state stand trial, when Laurent Gbagbo, the former president of Côte d'Ivoire, was indicted on four counts. He is alleged to have ordered the systematic murder, torture and rape of hundreds of political opponents in the wake of the 2010 Ivorian presidential election.

'Judge yourselves, not us!'

The accusation that the ICC is biased against Africans in nothing but a pretext. The truth is that quite a few of the current rulers of African states live in fear of being brought to trial themselves sooner or later. A prosecution has already been brought against one who is now a sitting president: in 2011 Uhuru Kenyatta was indicted by the ICC for crimes against humanity allegedly perpetrated during a spate of communal violence following the presidential election in Kenya in 2007–8. Despite being the subject of an arrest warrant, Kenyatta was himself elected president on 9 April 2013. Proceedings against him in The Hague were dropped in December 2014, after a succession of witnesses retracted their statements against him. Suspicions were raised that they had been induced to do so by threats or bribes.[148] 'Judge yourselves, not us!' Ugandan president Yoweri Museveni told the international community in an interview with the German news magazine *Der Spiegel* in June 2016.[149] Like Kenyatta, Museveni is in favour of setting up

a separate African court of human rights, 'financed and promoted by Africans'. In 2014 the heads of state of the AU signed
an agreement to this effect, but since then almost nothing has
happened. To date, not a single African parliament has ratified
the treaty.[150]

There is a glimmer of hope, however: in May 2016 the
Extraordinary African Chambers (Chambres Africaines
Extraordinaires, or CAE), a special tribunal of the AU, brought
one of the most brutal despots in the history of Africa to book.
For 23 years, Hissène Habré, the former president of Chad from
1982 to 1990, who had been responsible for the deaths of up to
40,000 people, had been living undisturbed in the Senegalese
capital Dakar. Representatives of his victims and human rights
organisations had been fighting for years to bring him to trial.
Their tenacity ultimately paid off. In 2015 Habré was finally
taken to court – in the very country that had sheltered him for
so many years. A class action was brought against him in Dakar
in the name of 4,445 survivors of the terror he unleashed and
relatives of his victims. After a trial lasting just under a year, the
tribunal found Habré guilty of war crimes and crimes against
humanity – including sexual slavery, forced abduction and rape
– and sentenced him to life imprisonment. Habré thus became
the first president to be tried and found guilty in the name of
Africa and on African soil.[151] Many Africans hope that this will
send out a powerful signal and that further prosecutions will
follow, in order to bring home to their rulers the realisation
that they do not have carte blanche, and that on the African
continent, too, crimes committed by heads and states of government will not go unpunished.

The crippling disunity afflicting the African Union was
demonstrated once more by the wrangling over the post of
chairperson of the AU Commission that took place at the

summit in Kigali in July 2016. The heads of state were unable to agree on a successor to the outgoing chairperson, Nkosazana Dlamini-Zuma of South Africa. None of the three female candidates for the position – from Equatorial Guinea, Uganda and Botswana, respectively – received the necessary two-thirds of votes. None of the 53 heads of state and government of the AU has so far seen fit to put forward a person of real stature, who is known and respected beyond the borders of their own country, for the most important post in their organisation.[152]

Voting with their feet

The people of Africa long for freedom and an end to oppression and injustice. Above all they are searching for their place in the Africa of tomorrow – and that is especially true of the continent's many young inhabitants. If there is any one thing that unites the youth of Africa today it is their hunger for knowledge and opportunity. They want to go to school, and perhaps even to university. They look forward to one day earning enough money to start a family. And they wish to have a say in determining the destiny of their countries. But all that is beyond the reach of most of the ambitious young people living in Africa's teeming cities. They can see how something new is springing up all around them, but they are not part of it. If African leaders continue to refuse to give their citizens a stake in society, they will surely lose the hearts and minds of their people. If they keep denying them the rule of law, free and fair elections and the right of co-determination, Africans will vote with their feet: they will turn their back on the continent and set off in search of a brighter future elsewhere. Many are doing so already, most notably in those countries with harsh authoritarian rule.

Eritrea: 'Everyone wants to leave'

In Eritrea, where the situation is particularly dire, people are leaving the country in droves. In 2016, the UNHCR counted more than 430,000 Eritreans who had turned their back on their homeland.[153] Relative to its overall population of just 5 million, this figure puts Eritrea among the African countries experiencing the greatest exodus of people. In 2014, 37,000 Eritreans made it across the Mediterranean to Europe, while another 40,000 took this route in 2015. In addition, around 120,000 of their compatriots are languishing in refugee camps in the neighbouring countries of Ethiopia and Sudan. Yet this mass flight from the country began as far back as the start of the millennium. In 2002, the Eritrean government introduced indefinite national service. Millions of Eritreans found themselves forced to do military or civilian service for the state – a system of organised corvée labour. Everyone between the ages of 18 and 50, of either sex, is liable to be drafted. The state decides in what role and for how long people are employed, be it as soldiers, teachers or labourers in the state construction firm. In return they receive starvation wages, often amounting to as little as 500 nafka, or just €30, a month.

Since the country gained its independence from Ethiopia in 1993, it has been led by Isaias Afewerki, formerly a rebel leader and now secretary-general of the state party, the People's Front for Democracy and Justice. There is no opposition, and the country is governed under a permanent state of emergency. The constitution, passed in 1997, was never enacted and the elections, scheduled for 2001, have never been held.[154] Eritreans live in the stranglehold of a system of repression and fear implemented by the secret service, the military and police-state surveillance. Torture and arbitrary detentions are commonplace. The country's university was closed in 2005. There is only one state-controlled television station and private newspapers are banned. On the World Press Freedom Index published by the organisation Reporters Without Borders, Eritrea has for many years come bottom, or second-to-bottom, of the list, rivalled only by North Korea in its repressiveness.[155]

Small wonder, then, that most young Eritreans wish only to get out of the country as quickly as they can. 'Everyone wants to leave, no one wants to stay' is a sentiment I hear over and over again among Eritreans in exile. Without this diaspora, Eritrea's economy would long since have collapsed. All Eritreans resident abroad are obliged to pay the state a 'recovery and reconstruction tax' of 2 per cent of their gross income – irrespective of whether they are earning an income or living on welfare payments. As a general rule, this tax is collected through Eritrea's embassies and consulates in the respective countries. In 2011 this practice was outlawed by the EU, but the Eritrean government has found a new way of levying the tax: all Eritrean nationals living abroad are now required to travel to the country or to instruct a relation within Eritrea to hand over the tax. Anyone refusing to comply is threatened with reprisals. They are denied official accreditation and basic consular services, and their relatives living in Eritrea are subject to persecution.[156]

Altogether, the 'recovery and reconstruction tax' raised from around a million Eritreans in the diaspora, plus aid donations and other contributions, make up a third of the state's budget.[157] Even larger are the sums sent from abroad to dependents at home, who find it impossible to live on the meagre income they get from national service. And so the contributions of Eritreans living in exile have helped in a major way to prop up the regime. Publicly, Afewerki condemns the exodus of his people and accuses Europe of having lured them away through their generous asylum provision. But, in actual fact, Afewerki can have little interest in stemming the tide of those leaving. For one thing, it rids him of potential trouble-makers – and the diaspora tax and steady flow of funds from abroad are the only things sustaining his murderous regime.

The brain drain in Zimbabwe

The situation for the people of Zimbabwe also appears particularly desperate. Over the course of his 37-year rule from 1980 to 2017, the country's dictator Robert Mugabe drove a third of his populace abroad. Zimbabwe's economic situation is now catastrophic, with unemployment running at over 90 per cent. At one time, Zimbabwe was Africa's breadbasket, exporting grain and meat to its neighbours. Today its people are starving and living in grinding poverty. This is primarily the result of the so-called land reform, which in reality was no more than a systematic campaign of dispossession. The farms of white settlers were seized and occupied, and their former owners expelled, in clandestine and often violent raids. For the most part, the expropriated land was turned over not, as Mugabe propagandised, to landless Zimbabwean farmers, but to people with good connections to the ruling party ZANU-PF. Agricultural productivity fell dramatically, and large tracts of land lay fallow. The country's hospitals ran out of essential supplies. Many people are now dying of malaria and diarrhoea, and around 15 per cent of 15- to 40-year-olds have been infected with HIV. Mugabe's most effective instrument of government was fear; he controlled the army, the police and the state security service. Especially feared is the Fifth Brigade, a special military unit that has been responsible for many atrocities against the civilian population. Its members were once trained in North Korea.

In the meantime, the people of Zimbabwe ceased to give any credence to Mugabe's mantra-like assertions that everything would be all right if only the whites were driven from the country. In particular, the managerial class and better-educated Zimbabweans quit the country in their thousands – business graduates, engineers, skilled workers, academics, doctors and nurses. By 2017, 2.5 million Zimbabweans were living in South Africa and 250,000 in Botswana. More than half a million are trying to build new lives for themselves in the old colonial mother country of Great Britain. This brain drain has had a disastrous effect on the economy: the number of potential employers is dwindling all the time, meaning correspondingly fewer jobs. The healthcare system has all but collapsed. There are currently more Zimbabwean doctors and nurses in London than in their home country. Only one sector is booming: mobile phone companies. This is because payments from Zimbabweans abroad are mostly made via e-transfers using cellphones. In common with many other African states, Zimbabwe is being kept alive on a drip feed of funds provided by its émigré citizens. Without their money transfers, the country would cease to be viable.[158]

In autumn 2015, the ageing Mugabe signalled his intention to stand for office once more in the elections due to be held in 2018 – but in November 2017 he was toppled from power by a military coup. Mugabe announced that he was stepping down as president, and his former vice president Emmerson Mnangagwa, a long-standing 'strongman' in the ruling ZANU-PF party, was sworn in as the country's new leader. At his inauguration, Mnangagwa proclaimed a 'new democracy', yet to date there is little to indicate that these words will be backed up by deeds.

The dream of Europe

The brain drain is evident in many African countries that have found their populations haemorrhaging abroad, such as Nigeria. Most of the well-educated people who have emigrated have no intention of returning to their homeland any time soon. Their primary aim is to start a new life abroad and to assume the nationality of their host country. Well-educated Nigerians emigrate principally to the US, Great Britain and the Gulf States. Yet the worsening political and economic situation in Nigeria also drove, and continues to drive, less well educated people abroad as well.[159] The UNHCR recorded 68,200 people as having left Nigeria in 2015.[160]

Throughout the whole of West Africa – in Mali, Niger, Guinea, Senegal and elsewhere – young people in particular are showing a greater propensity to turn their backs on their home countries.[161] They own smartphones, surf the internet, use social media and are perfectly well aware of the prosperity in which people in other parts of the world live. And while, in the first decade of the twenty-first century, the dream destination for many West Africans was South Africa, most now think of Europe as the most attractive option – though not the only one. Before they set off, many of them take out a loan, or the family makes a collection for them, to cover transport costs and payments to traffickers. For those left behind, it is an investment in the future. They hope that, if one of their relatives makes it to Europe, she or he will be able to support them by sending money. Countless young Africans who are turned back at Europe's borders, or whose application for asylum is turned down, simply try again – none of them have anything to lose.

African heads of state and government respond to this mass exodus of their young, intelligent and industrious citizens with a collective shrug of the shoulders. Many of them no doubt would like to imagine that this is a way of ridding themselves of malcontents and rebels. They refuse to register the fact that discontent is now endemic throughout Africa, and that the longer this frustration is allowed to build, the greater the likelihood it will erupt in rage sometime, somewhere. They say nothing about their compatriots dying of exhaustion on treks across the desert or drowning in the Mediterranean. While half of Europe is racking its brains over what to do about the refugee crisis, African leaders have thus far not deemed it necessary to call an emergency summit to discuss the plight of refugees. This is scarcely surprising when one bears in mind that it was Robert Mugabe who held the presidency of the African Union in 2015; to examine the problem in any shape or form would have entailed sitting in judgement on himself. 'Africa's presidents know full well that they dare not call on their people to stop emigrating,' explains Father Étienne, a priest from Niger who cares for the flood of refugees passing through his country on their way across the Sahara. 'They'd have a revolution on their hands. The people would retort: "Well then, it's up to you to make sure that there is enough work for us at home."'[162]

Now that the West has seen at first hand the catastrophic results of African leaders' policies, criticism of their failures has grown louder. At the February 2016 Munich Security Conference, which was convened to discuss the situation in Africa, the former UN Secretary-General Kofi Annan did not mince his words: 'Leaders who show more concern for the protection of their peers than the protection of their people are fanning the flames of righteous indignation.' Following Annan's speech, the Secretary-General of Amnesty International Salil Shetty addressed the meeting: 'We have a refugee crisis, a humanitarian crisis and in some cases even a security crisis. But above all, it seems we have a leadership crisis [...] Virtually all of these humanitarian crises are predictable and many of them prevent-able... [They] have their origins in governments suppressing freedoms of their people.'[163] And in Washington, President Barack Obama had also declared, on the occasion of the United States–Africa Leaders Summit of August 2014: 'Africa doesn't need strong men, it needs strong institutions.' But these fine words were not backed up with deeds. The West continued as before to place a premium on supposed stability and lucrative business rather than on the rule of law and human rights. So it is that Ethiopia is regarded by the West as an 'anchor of stabil-ity' in the region and an indispensable partner in containing radical Islamists in the Horn of Africa. A while ago, a British diplomat confided to the Africa correspondent of the Swiss newspaper the *Neue Zürcher Zeitung*: 'Just as long as thousands of people aren't gunned down in the streets of Addis Ababa, Great Britain will support the Ethiopian government.'[164]

The autocratic governments of Rwanda and Burundi also continue to receive unswerving support from the West because they too have pledged to join the War on Terror. Burundi con-tributed several thousand troops to the UN-backed Amisom mission in Somalia; for its part Rwanda provided more than 3,000 'blue helmet' soldiers to the peacekeeping mission in Darfur in Sudan. And even politicians like Denis Sassou Nguesso from the Republic of Congo enjoy strong backing in the Western world. After all, he controls the considerable deposits of oil and other minerals in his country. The same applies to José Eduardo dos Santos, who has wielded presiden-tial power in Angola since 1979, despite the fact that Angola regularly tops the list of the world's most corrupt states.

In South Africa, the largest democracy on the African con-tinent, municipal elections took place in August 2016. There was a groundswell of discontent in the country, even among the supporters of the African National Congress (ANC), the party of Nelson Mandela, which had held power since the end of apartheid. The unemployment rate stood at 27 per cent and economic growth had stagnated. But what particularly incensed a lot of South Africans was the autocratic posturing of their president Jacob Zuma, who had held the presidency since 2009. Corruption allegations mounted against him. In the spring of 2016 the country's supreme court had ruled that the president had violated the constitution by having his private luxury villa in Nkandla built with state funds, misappropriating millions of dollars of taxpayers' money in the process. A record number of South African voters – 26.3 million – had registered for the local elections. Voting was free and fair and passed off peacefully. For the first time in its history, the ANC suffered a bitter setback. In the large cities especially, the ruling party lost majorities which it had thought were rock-solid, and was forced to cede control to the liberal opposition party the Democratic Alliance.[165] The poll was proof positive that democracy was alive and well in South Africa. Then, in August 2017, Zuma faced a parliamentary motion of no confidence in him, the first to be held by secret ballot. He survived, but only just.

In many cities in Africa – Johannesburg, Cape Town and Pretoria as well as Lagos, Nairobi, Dakar and Addis Ababa – a generation is growing up that is increasingly finding its political voice. Young people are frustrated at their governments' incompetence and the sense of utter stagnation in their countries. A youth movement known as Y'en a Marre ('Fed up!') was founded in 2011 in the Senegalese capital Dakar, and gained huge popularity there. Young people in Senegal were no longer prepared to put up with a youth unemployment rate of almost 50 per cent and a situation where 400,000 university graduates were unable to find jobs.[166] Their protest, which was supported by popular singers and rappers, was instrumental in ensuring that the controversial long-serving president Abdoulaye Wade failed in his unconstitutional bid to secure a third term in office in early 2012. In a run-off against the opposition candidate Macky Sall on 26 March of that year, the 85-year-old Wade was forced to concede defeat. The elections in Senegal were hailed as a seminal lesson in democracy in Africa, and at the time many young Africans told themselves: 'We are all Senegalese now.'[167]

Many of Africa's youth of today have followed news of the Arab Spring revolts with great interest and sympathy. They are asking themselves: should they stay and fight for a better future in their own countries, or should they, like so many of their friends and acquaintances, flee abroad? They demand prosperity, democracy and breathing space. And they ask themselves whether they can count on the support of Europe and the West in their struggle, or whether they will be left in the lurch. Either way, they will come to their decision. Africa is always good for a surprise.

4

EUROPE'S RESPONSIBILITY

'We can do it!' declared the German federal chancellor Angela Merkel in September 2015 – and her chancellorship has thereafter been identified with this phrase like no other. The images of that summer are imprinted on many people's minds; hundreds of thousands of refugees had landed in Greece and Italy – so many that the authorities were completely overwhelmed by the influx. And so they allowed the migrants to move on. The resulting scenes were of a kind that had not been witnessed in Western Europe for 70 years. At the sight of the endless processions of people trekking from one frontier to the next, many observers were reminded of the people of Israel in their exodus from Egypt. In Budapest, thousands of stranded migrants camped for weeks on the underground level of the Eastern Railway Station – and the whole time the authorities there made no attempt to supply them with water, food or adequate toilet facilities. At their wits' end, some of these people lay down on the railway tracks in protest at their plight and were beaten with truncheons by the Hungarian police for their pains.

On the morning of 4 September 2015, more than 1,000 refugees set out from Budapest to walk the 175 kilometres to the border with Austria. By nightfall, they had covered a distance of 30 kilometres along the motorway, with traffic thundering past them the whole time. That night, Merkel took the decision to allow the desperate refugees to migrate to Germany, and special trains were laid on. When, shortly after, the question of whether Germany ought to close the border with Austria arose, the chancellor decided against this course of action – eschewing the advice of her interior minister and the head of the federal police.[168] For a while, the borders of Europe were wide open. Hundreds of thousands of refugees streamed into Austria and Germany.

Germany's welcoming culture

Germany showed the refugees a welcoming face. While the country's parliamentarians were still in their summer recess, the citizens on the ground took matters into their own hands. All over the country, temporary accommodation was set up, beds and mobile toilets were procured, and food kitchens were organised. Thousands of volunteers offered their services, collecting clothes, toys, food parcels, nappies and medicines, distributing blankets and bottled water and providing the new arrivals with essentials. The migrants, utterly exhausted by their months of aimless wandering, were greeted with applause at railway stations. Small children, their eyes wide with disbelief, had teddy bears pressed into their hands, and in many places placards were waved bearing the message – in English – 'Refugees Welcome!' In no time, gyms were emptied and turned into makeshift dormitories. Hundreds of action groups and other organisations were involved in the aid effort, organising donation collections, setting up cafés to feed the refugees and accompanying the new arrivals on visits to government offices. A German word began doing the rounds in the Anglo-Saxon world: *willkommenskultur*.

This hospitality was not confined to Germany; in places like Austria and Sweden, too, the refugees were received with open arms. Merkel politely but firmly dismissed criticism of this policy, not only from abroad but also from senior politicians from her own camp – notably the Christian Social Union, the Bavarian sister party of the Christian Democratic Union (CDU). At a press conference with Werner Faymann, who was then the Austrian chancellor, she announced: 'I must say quite honestly that if we now feel we have to start apologising for showing a friendly face in dire situations, then I don't recognise my country anymore.'[169] Many people really did believe that Germany's actions would set an example throughout Europe, and that the other countries of the EU would start taking their share of responsibility for the refugees. There was genuine hope that a new era of humane and generous policies toward refugees might be dawning.

Europe disunited

A year later, the new 'welcoming culture' in Europe had all but evaporated. Frontiers were reasserted, and a policy of deterrence was once more the order of the day. Germany's erstwhile allies had rowed back from their former support. Sweden, for instance, which in 2015 had taken in some 163,000 refugees, closed its borders in November of that year and tightened up its asylum legislation. Germany's neighbour Austria made it known that it could not accept any more than 37,500 refugees in 2016. The Central European states of the Visegrád Group (Poland, the Czech Republic, Slovakia and Hungary) came out in strong opposition to a plan to distribute refugees across the member states of the EU. Other states also showed themselves less than supportive. It was only with great difficulty that the reallocation of 120,000 refugees across the member states of the EU over a period of two years could be agreed upon. On top of the Czech Republic, Hungary, Romania and Slovakia voting against this measure, a majority of member countries rejected a permanent and binding allocation formula. One such nation was France, whose head of government Manuel Valls announced in February 2016 that his country could not take any more than the agreed 30,000 refugees.[170] The whole of Europe witnessed the rise of populist right-wing parties, which were fundamentally opposed to taking in migrants, and which put their respective countries' governments under great pressure. These included the Front National in France, the Sverigdemokraterna (Swedish Democrats), the Danske Folkeparti (Danish People's Party) and the Freiheitliche Partei Österreichs (Freedom Party of Austria).

In Germany itself, too, the cheerful and optimistic mood of autumn 2015 gave way to a more sombre attitude. The sheer magnitude of the huge effort involved – on both a financial and a logistical level – in not only housing a million refugees in the long term but also integrating them became clear to policymakers only gradually. Events such as the assaults carried out against young women by young men of North African origin during the New Year celebrations in Cologne in 2015, and the terror attacks that took place in Würzburg and Ansbach in the summer of 2016, hardened people's attitudes against taking in new migrants. In both of the latter cases, the perpetrators – who claimed allegiance to the Islamist terror group IS (Islamic State, or Daesh) – had entered the country as refugees. At the same time, attacks against migrant shelters increased alarmingly. The Alternative für Deutschland (Alternative for Germany) movement, which put the refugee question front and centre of its campaign, made unexpected advances in local and regional polls in both the east and west of the country from 2015 onwards, and in the national elections of September 2017 it secured almost 6 million votes and won 94 seats in the Bundestag – the first far-right representation in the German parliament since the Second World War. Nevertheless, many thousands of people continue to campaign for a more open society, and to be involved in action groups and other organisations caring for the welfare of the new arrivals.

The politics of migration and the refugee question appear to be making Europe an ever more divided continent. In a June 2016 referendum, a narrow majority of Britons (52 to 48 per cent) voted for the proposition that the UK should leave the EU. The question of immigration to the UK was one of the key issues in this acrimonious campaign. 'Brexit' acted like a beacon to a EU where centrifugal forces appear to be in the ascendant. The refugee question clearly exposed the current parlous state of European solidarity; the likelihood of member states adopting a common policy on this subject now appears more remote than ever. Some administrations even seem willing to abandon precisely those values that constitute the whole idea of European unity. 'Ugly incidents will be bound to occur,' stated Sebastian Kurz (then the Austrian foreign minister and subsequently, as of December 2017, the country's chancellor) in reference to violent scuffles on the Macedonian border, where the police used water cannons against women and children. Openly flouting the provisions of the 1951 Refugee Convention, Kurz has argued that EU states should 'start preventing refugees from entering and refusing any further asylum applications'.[171] He maintains that the EU should take a leaf out of Australia's policy on refugees, which would mean that any migrants who did not arrive in Europe by legal means would forfeit their right to claim asylum. If it were to prove impractical to immediately send them back to their countries of origin, Kurz's preferred solution would be to intern them temporarily, 'ideally on an island'.[172] The Australian navy is well known for systematically turning back boats containing refugees. Those migrants who still make it ashore are detained in internment camps on the Pacific island of Nauru, and on the island of Manus in Papua New Guinea. Australia's policy on refugees has come under repeated criticism from the UN for being inhumane – and with good reason: in August 2016, documents came to light showing that assaults, sexual abuse and suicide attempts form part of the daily routine in the camps on Nauru.[173] After the Supreme Court of Papua New Guinea ruled that internment on Manus Island was unconstitutional, the Australian government announced on 17 August 2016 that the detention camp there would be closed. Well over a year later, in October 2017, the camp was finally closed. The inmates were transported by police units to three new detention centres in Papua New Guinea, near the provincial capital of Lorengau. The construction of these was financed by the Australian government. Nevertheless, Australia continues to refuse to receive the refugees interned there. The international aid organisation Médecins Sans Frontières was refused access to the new successor camps.[174] Anyone seriously putting forward the Australian experience as a model for European immigration policy has clearly long since renounced the principles of the rule of law and humane conduct.

The system of compartmentalisation

In the countless discussions of the refugee crisis that have taken place, the demand has repeatedly been made that Europe should resolve once and for all to tackle the 'causes of mass migration'. There is scarcely a leading European politician who has not espoused this imperative and made it his or her own. Aside from the Middle East, the focus is increasingly alighting upon Africa. At an economic summit of the CDU in Berlin in June 2016, Merkel declared: 'We must deal with the question of Africa [...] The central problem is the migration of 1.2 billion people from Africa.'[175] Yet the steps that Europe is about to take tell a different tale. As of autumn 2016, Europe is preparing to return to that system of compartmentalisation that has always been the traditional European approach to refugee policy. For several decades, Europe operated according to the principle of 'a refugee is only a good refugee in my neighbour's garden'. Yet with the signing of the Schengen Agreement, concluded on 14 June 1985, the governments of Belgium, Germany, France, Luxembourg and the Netherlands undertook to henceforth dispense with all controls on the borders between them. In 1997 the Schengen Agreement was incorporated into EU law – with only Denmark, Great Britain and Ireland obtaining exception clauses. Closely associated with the Schengen Area were rulings concerning the common securing of the external borders of the EU. With regard to granting the right to asylum, EU member states agreed upon the so-called Dublin Regulation, according to which the European country where an asylum seeker first sets foot is responsible for processing his or her application for asylum. Within the EU each asylum claim can only be considered once. If it is turned down, the asylum seeker cannot submit a new application in another member state. For countries in the centre of the EU and without any borders to non-EU countries – such as Germany – this was a very practical ruling, which ensured that for many years the numbers of asylum seekers were kept reliably low. Conversely, the main burden was borne by those countries on the periphery of the EU, primarily Italy and Greece.

Right from the outset, the 'Dublin system' was bedevilled by the fact that not even remotely the same standards apply across the board in the EU when dealing with asylum seekers. The criteria according to which people are granted asylum have always differed widely between individual EU countries, and still do. Accordingly, an asylum seeker from Afghanistan's chance of having his application approved are 10 times higher in Sweden than they are in Greece.[176] Also, certain EU countries have been criticised time and again as regards the provision of housing for migrants. Amnesty International has accused Hungary and Bulgaria of routinely throwing asylum seekers in gaol. In January 2011, the European Court of Human Rights in Strasbourg refused to sanction the return to Greece of migrants who had entered the EU via that country before travelling on to other countries, on the grounds that they ran the risk of facing 'humiliating and inhumane treatment' there.[177]

'Airtight' borders

The huge influx of refugees into Europe in the summer of 2015 brought the Dublin system to a de facto state of collapse, and the principle of free movement throughout Europe hung in the balance. Toll gates and border controls returned to Europe – something that the Schengen Agreement had only envisaged in exceptional circumstances, and even then only for a period of six months at most. In Hungary and Slovenia, border fences were even put in place once more. The frontiers of Europe were to be sealed and made 'airtight', declared the Hungarian prime minister Viktor Orbán in March 2016.[178] To deal with the flood of refugees entering Greece and Italy, mobile 'hotspot' reception centres, where EU officials and local authorities could register the new incomers, were to be established.

The European border protection agency Frontex, which was created by the EU in 2004, was set to play a leading role in securing its external borders. The original purpose of this agency was simply to coordinate protection of the EU external frontier between the member states. However, over the years it has developed into a kind of European border police with its own surveillance apparatus – notwithstanding the fact that the securing of external borders continues to be the responsibility of the individual states. Frontex's operational capacities have been steadily expanded, while its budget has increased from €19.2 million in 2006 to €114 million in 2015.[179] Frontex monitors ports and uses its patrol boats to try and halt and refugee vessels and force them to turn back before they reach the coasts of Europe. Emergency rescue at sea is expressly not part of its remit. The EU has left its member states on the maritime periphery to their own devices in this regard. Between October 2013 and 2014, under the auspices of Operation Mare Nostrum (meaning Our Sea), the Italian navy rescued more than 150,000 people from the Mediterranean Sea.[180] This action was a thorn in the side of many European politicians: saving shipwrecked refugees, it was argued, would only encourage more migrants to attempt the sea crossing to Europe in unseaworthy vessels. The successor project, coordinated by Frontex and named after the Greek sea god Triton, is therefore strictly confined to the inshore coastal waters of Italy and is moreover far less well equipped than Operation Mare Nostrum.

In July 2016, the European Parliament in Strasbourg approved the EU plan to transfer even more powers to Frontex, including the right if need be to undertake operations along the external frontiers of the Schengen Area, even without the agreement of the member states. It is envisaged that the agency will eventually have 1,000 regular employees along with a rapid-deployment reserve of 1,500 border guards, who can be mobilised within three days.[181] In addition, the EU is pouring even more investment into the surveillance of its land and sea borders. By means of the European border surveillance system Eurosur, introduced in 2013, the monitoring of the continent's external frontiers with the aid of data banks, satellite technology, high-resolution cameras, drones and biometrics will, it is hoped, be honed to a state of technical perfection. An amount of €244 million was ring-fenced from the budget of the EU for implementation and maintenance of the system up to 2020.[182] To date, the EU has pumped a total of €2 billion into the upgrading and technological development of a 'smart' border – a massive investment programme for the international armaments and security industry.[183] The sole purpose of this 'Big Brother' system is to make it practically impossible for refugees to reach Europe. For example, drones could alert the authorities in Algeria or Libya, enabling them to intercept groups of refugees on their territories and send them home long before they ever reach Europe's external border.

Europe's 'partner' Gaddafi

For many years, the EU could rely on other countries bearing the brunt of the effort of securing its external borders. In North Africa, the regimes of Zine el-Abidine Ben Ali in Tunisia and Muammar Gaddafi in Libya did Europe's dirty work for it. Tunisia, for example, outlawed 'illegal emigration' to Europe. From 2003 onwards, numerous camps were built in both countries for the internment of refugees who were trying to make their way to Europe. Many of these camps were run under extremely inhumane conditions – and the EU rewarded the governments of the Maghreb handsomely for their efforts in keeping Africa's migrants away from Europe. In 2004, the EU approved the lifting of economic sanctions and the arms embargo against Libya. In particular, Italy – where most refugees from Africa had always made land – was a keen advocate of this deal. The Italian foreign minister at the time, Franco Frattini, justified his country's stance by claiming that Libya was being equipped with 'the necessary tools' to conduct effective patrols along its land and sea borders in order to prevent illegal immigration.[184] Italy declared Libya, where people's human rights were being trampled underfoot, to be a 'safe third country' and put billions of euros at the disposal of the regime for the purposes of 'refugee control'. The services of the 'partner' Gaddafi were highly prized not just in Italy but also right across the EU at this time; he was seen as a guarantor of stability in the region.

In 2011, however, all this came to an abrupt end. First, in January, the Tunisian dictator Ben Ali was swept from office by the Jasmine Revolution, and a few weeks later the Arab Spring also reached Libya, plunging the country into civil war. In October 2011, Gaddafi was captured by rebel forces and executed. At a stroke, the EU had lost its most important 'partners' in maintaining the security of its external borders.

New dirty deals

In front of the cameras and microphones, Europe's politicians were keen to stress the existential necessity of combatting the causes of mass migration. Behind the scenes, though, they appeared primarily concerned with short-term crisis management: new dirty deals with dubious partners were designed to ensure that people from the Middle East and Africa seeking refuge would also in future be kept away from Europe. The treaty on refugees signed by the EU with Turkey, mainly at the German government's instigation, marked the beginning of this development. Under this agreement, the EU granted the Turkish president €6 million and various political concessions in return for his government agreeing to take back refugees who had arrived in Greece through Turkish territory. In addition, it was agreed that, for every Syrian deported from Greece back to Turkey, another Syrian refugee would be allowed to emigrate legally from Turkey into the EU. This deal, which came into force on 18 March 2016, had an immediate effect, cutting the daily influx of refugees and other migrants crossing to Greece from the Turkish coast from a peak of around 2,000 in February 2016 to just a few dozen in April.[185] Human rights organisations such as Amnesty International protested in the strongest terms against the agreement, calling it a clear violation of international law. Turkey could not, in the opinion of Salil Shetty, Amnesty International's secretary-general, be considered a safe country of origin, as the refugees living there had no secure legal status. They had neither the option, he maintained, of gaining permanent residency in Turkey nor the genuine prospect of being settled in another host country.[186] After the failed military coup of July 2016 and the enforced autocratic reshaping of Turkey under President Erdogan, the survival of the agreement appears more doubtful than ever.

In spite of this, the Turkish deal continues to serve the EU as a model for its accords with even more questionable partners in Africa. In November 2015, the EU resolved to set up an 'Emergency Trust Fund for stability and addressing root causes of irregular migration and displaced persons in Africa', to the tune of €1.8 billion. The potential partners listed are those African states which operate as the principal countries of origin and transit countries for migrants: Burkina Faso, Chad, The Gambia, Mauretania, Niger, Nigeria and Senegal in the Sahel zone and Chad Basin; Djibouti, Eritrea, Ethiopia, Kenya, Somalia, South Sudan, Sudan, Tanzania and Uganda in the Horn of Africa; and Morocco, Algeria, Tunisia, Libya and Egypt in North Africa. Among the objectives of the fund, the EU Commission identifies as a key target 'the effective sustainable return, readmission and reintegration of irregular migrants not qualifying for protection'. According to the Commission this is intended to foster 'a firm commitment to supporting capacity-building of third countries in the field of migration and border management, as well as to the stabilisation and development of these regions of Africa'.[187] Although several projects aimed at conflict prevention and boosting economic growth are indeed cited among those deemed worthy of promotion, the general tenor is nonetheless unmistakable: the fund's primary aim is to stop migration from Africa by any means possible. To finance the fund, the intention is above all to 'reallocate' resources from the European Development Fund, which has the stated aim of promoting development cooperation. This means that money originally earmarked for development aid and the strengthening of civil society is instead being used to finance border protection and to prop up autocratic regimes in Africa. Furthermore, the EU envisages further payments of billions of euros in connection with 'migration partnerships' with such countries as Tunisia, Nigeria, Senegal, Mali, Niger, Ethiopia and Libya; those countries which declare a willingness to further secure their borders and to take back illegal migrants from Europe are to be rewarded. The message is clear and unequivocal: 'We'll send you money as long as you don't send us any refugees.'[188]

A confidential document titled Sharm El Sheikh Plan of Action identifies Sudan and Eritrea in particular as cooperation partners. The basis for this is the so-called Khartoum Process, which was agreed among 58 European and African countries in 2014 with the objective of curbing migration.[189] On the part of the EU, the plan envisages 'reinforcing the personal and institutional capacities of the Eritrean government in the fight against people-trafficking and smuggling'. But does the EU really want to cooperate with a dictatorial government like that in Eritrea, and to even reward it for driving its own citizens out of the country through the inhumane policies it enacts? Does the EU really want to work with people like Sudan's President Omar al-Bashir, against whom there is an outstanding arrest warrant issued by the International Criminal Court in The Hague for suspected genocide and crimes against humanity in the Darfur region? At least according to the Sharm El Sheikh Plan of Action, a 'regional training centre for combatting people trafficking and smuggling of persons' will be set up in Sudan.[190] To date, the EU has already paid Eritrea €200 million to help fund a project 'combatting the causes of migration'. The money is intended to be channelled into the development of the energy sector and improvements in electricity distribution. The Eritrean head of state Isaias Afewerki has indicated that, in return, he will reduce the country's widely hated 'national service' period to 18 months. He has promised this already several times in connection with prospective aid money. He has never kept this promise, however.[191] Indeed, why should he want to change anything about the existing situation when the money he extorts from exiled Eritreans, in the form of the 'recovery and reconstruction tax', has become one of the state's principal revenue streams?

Other African countries, too, have found that their refugees and migrants abroad represent a lucrative source of income, Niger, for example, numbers among the poorest countries in the world. In the 2016 Human Development Index issued by the UN, the country was in second-to-last place (prior to this it repeatedly occupied the final spot).[192] Here, the smuggling of migrants has become an important sector of the economy. Almost all of those who leave West Africa with an eye to emigrating to Europe pass through the desert state. Agadez in the north of the country has become the capital of the people smugglers. The Sahara begins immediately outside the city, and on the far side of the desert lies Libya. Many of Agadez's 120,000 inhabitants have meanwhile come to earn their living from the migrants – not only the people smugglers, but also the providers of accommodation, auto traders who sell them cars and even roadside vendors who offer the migrants water at inflated prices. No fewer than seven banks have opened branches in the city in recent years; these are used by dozens of small traders for currency exchanges of cash. Human trafficking is now estimated to account for more than half of all economic activity in Agadez.[193] The country's police and armed forces also earn a tidy sum from this industry. It is therefore hardly surprising that the authorities in Niger show little inclination to drain this lucrative source of wealth.

Niger's president Mahamadou Issoufou had for some time been assiduously courted by Europe: it is the EU's intention that he should halt the transit of people through the territory he governs. At the EU's urging, Niger passed a law against people smuggling in 2015. However, this failed to reduce the flow of refugees and migrants – quite the opposite, in fact: by the summer of 2016, 16,000 migrants were passing through Agadez every week.[194] In May 2016, the German foreign minister at the time, Frank-Walter Steinmeier, visited Niamey, the capital of Niger. Just one month later, Chancellor Merkel received President Issoufou in Berlin. In their joint press conference, there was much talk of migration controls and border security. Issoufou declared his willingness to establish reception centres in his country, funded by the EU. However, there was no mention of how the state of Niger might be induced to offer its inhabitants any lasting prospects for the future.[195]

In the case of the Maghreb state of Mauretania, in the past the EU has demonstrated how such a 'migration treaty' functions in practice. Prior to 2006, hundreds of boats were arriving on the Canary Islands from this West African state. Subsequently, the EU and the Spanish government invested around €20 million in a programme of 'migration management'. This entailed the Spanish Guardia Civil and the Mauretanian security voices jointly patrolling the coast and preventing boats from leaving. Migrants who were intercepted found themselves interned for several years in a school that had been converted into a prison – which, thanks to the conditions there, and in allusion to the notorious American detention centre in Cuba, was dubbed 'Guantanamito'. From the millions of euros that flowed from Brussels and Madrid, the amount channelled into civilian initiatives to aid the refugees – only a trickle, some €160,000 all told – was a mere drop in the ocean.[196]

'The Khartoum Process has just one aim,' declared the head of the Brussels office of the organisation Human Rights Watch, Lotte Leicht, 'and that is to prevent refugees from reaching a coast from where they can attempt the crossing to Europe, and then to become a visible problem to us Europeans.'[197] In the interim, a broad front of resistance has lined up to oppose the EU's planned migration treaties with African states. Thus, in June 2016 a total of 104 international organisations – including Oxfam, Doctors of the World, Save the Children, World

Vision and Amnesty International – called on European heads of state and government to halt the plans of the EU and instead to 'develop a sustainable and long-term strategy' for organising migration.[198] Despite this, nothing has happened to suggest that there will be a change of direction on this policy. Quite the contrary, in fact: Germany, for instance, is planning to persuade North African countries beyond Morocco and Algeria to conclude bilateral treaties on the 'repatriation' of their nationals whose asylum applications have been turned down. In addition, it is the German government's intention to expand the list of so-called safe countries of origin. These include states 'in which, judging from the basis of the general political situation, it can reasonably be presumed that neither political persecution nor inhumane or demeaning punishment or treatment occurs,' in the words of the Federal Office for Migration and Refugees. Hitherto, the only African countries on this list have been Ghana and Senegal; now the plan is to add the Maghreb states of Algeria, Morocco and Tunisia. This would mean that people from those countries would have their right to seek asylum restricted. Their asylum applications will no longer be individually examined, and as a rule they will automatically be rejected as 'clearly unfounded'. Human rights organisations like Amnesty International are protesting against this plan, pointing in particular to the persecution of homosexuals and the systematic use of torture and other abuses that take place in these states.[199]

Rather than the causes of migration, it is the refugees themselves who are being combatted. In this situation, the measures aimed at compartmentalisation and strengthening border security have only proved a stimulus to the people smugglers: the more difficult it becomes to flee, the higher the price that the smugglers can charge. As a result of this, people will find even more dangerous ways of getting to their intended destination.

Freedom of movement? Not for Africans

Whenever there is talk of 'illegal' or 'irregular' migrants, one thing should always be borne in mind: for Africans there is virtually no possibility of emigrating to Europe by legal means. The freedom of movement that most Europeans take for granted simply does not exist for Africans. The majority of those who live in the Southern Hemisphere are prevented from moving around the world freely. For example, anyone from Ethiopia seeking to obtain a visa for the Schengen Area has to submit to a time-consuming and expensive bureaucratic procedure. He or she must state their reason for wishing to travel and prove that they will not pose a financial or other risk to their host country. In addition, they are required to present bank statements, a business licence or proof of income, a return ticket and valid health insurance documentation. It takes an outlay of several thousand euros to amass all the documents that are needed to get a visa. The requirements for issuing a visa to citizens of West African states like The Gambia are even more strict. European consulates there often demand that an applicant present letters of invitation from each host country he or she intends to visit, or declarations of surety for potential financial expenses.[200]

The following general trends have emerged. In recent years, the issuing of visas to Africans by European consulates has become subject to ever tighter restrictions – to the extent that this has become a serious impediment to business relations between Europe and Africa. Suspicious consular officials view almost every African applying for a visa as a potential 'offender' whose sole purpose is to surreptitiously secure long-term residency in Europe. Ultimately, all applicants are subject to the whims of bureaucracy: the granting of a visa can be denied without any requirement to reveal on what grounds it has been refused.

Younger, poorer and less well-educated people in Africa have a vanishingly small chance of ever being granted a visa to travel to Europe. Most of them fall at the first hurdle, failing to negotiate the bureaucratic labyrinth of application and assemble the various pieces of paperwork required for a visa. They will never be in a position to travel to Europe 'by legal means' – even if this were only to gain their own impression of living conditions there and then return to their own countries. All they have to go on are hearsay reports, the accounts of acquaintances or relatives and impressions gleaned from the television or social media. If, on the basis of all that, they decide to try and make their way to Europe, the only opportunity open to them is to stake everything on one roll of the dice – and risk their lives trying to make it to their destination as an 'illegal'.

In September 2015, the Agenda 2030 for Sustainable Development was passed at the UN General Assembly in New York. In this, the community of nations agreed on a 'treaty for the world's future', which was designed as a step towards ensuring that people worldwide might lead their lives in dignity. On the question of migration, Agenda 2030 states: 'We will cooperate internationally to ensure safe, orderly and regular migration involving full respect for human rights and the humane treatment of migrants regardless of migration status, of refugees and of displaced persons.'[201] It would appear, however, that this does not apply to Europe: instead of finally tackling the fundamental questions, the EU is instead hell-bent on simply curbing migration and shifting the security of its external frontiers into the Southern Hemisphere.

Unfair trade

Agenda 2030 is driven, as it clearly announces, by a spirit of 'new global partnership'. An integral part of this is a commitment to fair trade, as stated in paragraph 30 of the declaration:

> States are strongly urged to refrain from promulgating and applying any unilateral economic, financial or trade measures not in accordance with international law and the Charter of the UN that impede the full achievement of economic and social development, particularly in developing countries.[202]

This statement puts the finger on a glaring problem, for the one topic above all that the EU is desperate not to discuss where the question of Africa and migration is concerned is the scandalous agricultural and trade policies it conducts in order to cement global inequality firmly in place.

Year on year, export-oriented European agribusiness is supported by EU subsidies running into the billions of euros. More than 40 per cent of the EU's total budget is devoted to farming subvention – in 2014 alone, this amounted to over €40 billion in direct payments.[203] On top of this, there are also extensive export bonuses. This leads to a situation where European agribusiness floods developing countries with exceptionally cheap produce. Chicken is a prime example of this practice. Because large quantities of chicken thighs are unsaleable in Europe, where the greatest demand is for breast meat, producers have found new consumers on the neighbouring continent. There, Europe's unwanted poultry is dumped on the market at such low prices that African farmers find it impossible to compete. In 2014, the cost of producing one kilo of chicken meat in West Africa, which has been especially severely affected by cheap

EU exports, was €1.80, but European poultry was going on the market there at less than half that price. In spite of many years of criticism levelled at this unscrupulous practice, poultry exports from the EU to Africa nearly tripled between 2009 and 2014 – increasing from 200,000 to almost 600,000 tonnes.[204]

The devastating impact of the European policies of subvention and dumping can be seen almost everywhere in Africa. In Burkina Faso a few years ago, imports of cheap milk powder from the EU led to the majority of the country's nomadic small farmers losing their livelihood. They had been entirely dependent upon milk production to make a living. But the market for their milk vanished virtually overnight, after dairies in Burkina Faso switched to using the cheaper milk powder from Europe. At 30 cents per litre, the asking price for this product was not only markedly less than the production costs of European dairies, it also undercut costs of production within Burkina Faso by around 10 cents.[205]

In Ghana, importers of tomato puree from the EU have brought about the decline of indigenous tomato production. The huge influx of cheap tomato paste, chiefly from southern Italy, has put thousands of Ghanaian farmers out of business. They can no longer sell their produce, while in local markets, tomato puree cans from dozens of different brands, all labelled 'made in Italy', can be seen stacked in pyramids as tall as a man. Next to them, one can find breakfast cereals from Germany, tinned meat from Great Britain and milk powder from Denmark. European food manufacturers ship their subsidised goods to Africa by the tonne, thereby squeezing home-grown products out of the market. For example, Ghana annually imports some 50,000 tonnes of tomato puree from Italy.[206]

The situation in countries such as Ghana seems certain only to get worse in future, for the countries that banded together to form the Economic Community of West African States have recently, under massive pressure from the EU, signed a so-called Economic Partnership Agreement (EPA) with that organisation. This will further facilitate the import of European goods. Previously, Europe accorded these countries a special status; while European distributors were required to pay tariffs when exporting their goods to Africa, anyone seeking to export goods from Africa to Europe was exempt from all customs duties. Now, as part of the new agreement, African countries will be expected to also waive their tariffs on imports from the EU; the principle is that free trade should be paramount. But in the future, as before, it will continue to be anything but a trading arrangement between equals. 'We simply cannot compete with subsidised products,' maintains the Ghanaian economist Kwabena Otoo. 'Free trade between Europe and Africa is like a football match between Real Madrid and the Bole-Bamboi school team.'[207] In East Africa, where the EU has likewise negotiated an EPA with the East African Community, some stirrings of resistance have recently become apparent. In August 2016, Tanzania and Uganda announced that they would refuse to ratify the treaty.[208]

The trading policy of the EU has in the meantime been responsible for driving many former small farmers from Ghana to emigrate from their homeland. A large number of them have pitched up in Europe, some 46,500 of them in Italy alone. It is not without a certain bitter irony that many of them eke out a living there as low-paid agricultural labourers. In Apulia, which is home to vast tomato plantations, there is a run-down settlement near the town of Cerignola that is known as 'ghetto ghanese', the Ghanaian ghetto. During the harvesting season in the summer and autumn, the population of this shanty town swells to around 800.[209] Over 100,000 foreign pickers are employed in southern Italy. A large proportion of them are from Africa. Many have no papers, and have been character-ised as Italy's 'new slaves'. In return for a subsistence wage, they harvest the 'red gold', which then goes on to be exported to their home countries. As small cogs in the machine, they help maintain the very same system that caused them to lose their livelihoods at home and forced them to become economic migrants in the first place.

Hauls of fish off Africa's coast

The fisheries policy of the EU is also proving increasingly ruinous for Africa. For many people in countries like Somalia, The Gambia, Senegal or Sierra Leone, fish is an important food source thanks to its high nutritional value. But since huge trawlers and factory ships from Europe, Russia and Japan, and increasingly also from China, have started to appear off the coasts of Africa, this food resource is under threat. Industrial-scale fishing by global businesses deprives small African fishermen of their livelihoods and jeopardises the food supply of millions of people.[210]

Europe's fishery fleets around the world are supported by generous subsidies from Brussels; in 2012 the total sum involved was about €1 billion.[211] The seas of the Southern Hemisphere are lucrative fishing grounds, for there the catch quotas that are imposed by the EU have no force, applying as they do exclusively to the territorial waters of EU member states. Fisheries Partnership Agreements concluded by the EU with individual African countries have laid the groundwork for this exploitation of fish stocks. In Africa, such deals have been reached with Guinea-Bissau, Madagascar, Morocco and the Seychelles. In Mauretania, the EU has even secured unlimited access to the country's territorial waters in return for an annual payment of around €60 million.[212] Maximum catch levels have been set, but as yet no effective system of monitoring exists. A small proportion of the funds from Brussels, which have become one of the Mauretanian government's chief sources of foreign revenue – some €4 million annually – are earmarked for use in the development of a home-grown fishing industry. However, the bulk of the monies paid disappear into dark channels controlled by prominent supporters of the regime of General Mohamed Ould Abdel Aziz.

Where no bilateral agreements are in place, the situation is often even worse. For example, in 2006, Senegal terminated its fisheries treaty with the EU. The European fishery multinationals reacted in their customary manner, purchasing fishing vessels flying the Senegalese flag on a grand scale and simply continuing to catch in the country's territorial waters. The only difference now was that there were no concessionary payments; accordingly, in 2014 the Senegalese government agreed to sign a new treaty with the EU. In the interim, the local fishing sector had collapsed. Worse still, West African fishing grounds as a whole are facing collapse, with stocks of the most important edible fish species having slumped by up to 75 per cent in recent years.[213]

In any case, in countries like Somalia, where state control has effectively broken down, the law of the jungle now holds sway. There, for want of any regulation, European fishing fleets simply go ahead and fish at will without any licence. 'Western ships catch in a single night as much as Somali fishermen would take in a year,' says Roger Middleton from the British foreign policy think tank Chatham House. According to estimates by the UN Food and Agriculture Organization (FAO), every year foreign vessels operating off the coast of Somalia catch fish to the value of $350 to $400 million.[214] African organisations have long been calling for international measures to combat illegal fishing activity. With regard to Europe, they demand the abolition of EU subvention for European fishing fleets, which are plundering Africa's fish stocks – at the cost of indigenous fishermen.

The original intention of farming and fishery subsidies paid by the EU or its predecessor organisations to member states was to safeguard domestic food production in those countries, but over the course of time they have come instead to serve the purpose of a ruinous crowding out of competition worldwide and have led to the collapse of entire sectors of the economy in Africa and Asia. This in turn has had the effect of making the states affected ever more dependent on the import of foodstuffs. Yet EU countries regard payment of subsidies to the domestic farming sector as sacrosanct – no government in Europe wants to take on the powerful farming lobby in its respective country. As a result, things carry on as usual, and in spite of all the public declarations about 'global partnerships' the system of unfair trade remains firmly in place.

Development aid – for whom?

Haven't the industrialised countries of the world – with Europe at their forefront – been acting in exemplary fashion on behalf of Africa for decades in the form of generous payments of overseas development aid? In 2015, EU countries provided around $73.5 billion in development aid, with the UK alone contributing $18.7 billion. This makes the UK the second-largest donor nation in the world, behind the US – though its contribution expressed as a percentage of gross national income (0.71 per cent) only just makes it over the threshold of 0.7 per cent that donor nations have pledged to the UN that they will provide. Around one-third of the payments go to multinational organisations such as the EU and the World Bank, with the rest going to the individual countries.[215]

Conservative estimates suggest that over the past 60 years around two trillion US dollars have flowed from the so-called developed countries of the world to the underdeveloped nations, with the majority of this aid going to Africa. Yet an increasing number of people have begun to enquire how it can be that, in spite of all this aid, the lives of Africans have barely improved over that same period. Attempts to find answers to this question have filled entire libraries.[216] During the Cold War, representatives of the two power blocs in the West and East paid handsomely for the allegiance of the ruling elites in a number of Southern Hemisphere countries. Nowadays, the term 'development aid' has largely been expunged from the official vocabulary of donor countries; instead, they prefer to talk of 'development cooperation'. Yet tangible strategic and economic interests continue to play a significant role in the supposedly selfless donations. Thus, all too frequently the benevolence of the donor country turns out to be a stimulus programme for its domestic economy. US legislation stipulates that the overwhelming preponderance of American food aid to Africa, to the tune of two billion dollars annually, be purchased from US farmers, processed by American manufacturers and delivered to its destination by American enterprises.[217] And China is by no means the only country that offers its 'development cooperation' primarily to those states with raw materials that it wishes to exploit for the benefit of its domestic industry.

Nor are private donor organisations immune from self-interested motives. Over time, the African continent has been covered by a close-knit web of organisations with tens of thousands of employees. Competition between them is intense. Each one needs to demonstrate its indispensability in order to keep public donations rolling in – regardless of whether its work is truly useful or not. The many aid workers hardly ever consider that the real purpose of their roles consists of ultimately making themselves redundant. Critics of development aid are fond of referring to the 'development industry'. What remains beyond dispute is that aid in Africa, currently estimated at some $57 billion annually, has become one of the continent's most significant economic sectors – the total turnover of which equals the output of the 20 poorest African countries put together.[218]

Even the best of intentions can have disastrous consequences: free food aid destroys the market for local farm produce. All too often development funds do not reach those for whom they were intended – especially when they are transferred as direct budgetary assistance. In the hands of ruling kleptocrats, this money becomes an instrument for maintaining a hold on power, and provides them with the wherewithal to sustain rampant corruption. A phrase often heard among Africa's elites is: 'You pretend to help us and we pretend to develop.' As long as this still holds true, nothing will ever change for the better in Africa.

In one respect above all, this dependence upon aid money has proved a complete disaster: it robs people of their individual initiative. Nowadays, the attitude has taken hold among a not inconsiderable number of Africans that others will solve their problems for them. But no country, and no human being, can ever regard it as dignified to be branded as an eternal recipient of handouts. One can therefore perfectly well understand the new generation of career-minded Africans who are raising their voices in protest at this state of affairs – like the entrepreneur Ola Orekunrin from Nigeria, who has said that she doesn't want to be 'saved' by anyone. This generation wants to be rescued least of all by those who once came to Africa as colonial masters but who now present themselves as Good Samaritans, and who, moreover, with their financial donations only succeed in keeping in power corrupt old men who have their own interests at heart. It is not only Western economists such as William Easterly of New York University or the Scottish Nobel Prize laureate Angus Deaton who now criticise development aid as being inappropriate and misguided; more and more Africans have now aligned themselves with the naysayers.[219] One of the first of these was Axelle Kabou from Cameroon, who studied economics in Paris. She herself worked for many years in the development sector and acted as an advisor to African presidents. After quitting her development role, she authored a polemic in 1991 entitled 'Et si l'Afrique refusait le développement?' (meaning 'and what if Africa refused development?').[220] At the heart of her critique lay the contention that Africa's 'black elites' were incapable of changing and that many Africans were unwilling to develop their continent through their own efforts. Today, numerous African intellectuals also think along these lines – such as Roger Tangri, George Ayittey and Chika Onyeani. Some of them, like the Kenyan economist James Shikwati, even go so far as to advocate the cessation of all development aid.[221]

Yet such radical and populist demands change nothing. By contrast, many aid workers in Africa are engaged in extremely worthwhile projects. It is also incontrovertibly the case that over the past few decades emergency aid has saved millions of Africans from dying of starvation. As the diplomat and long-serving German ambassador in Cameroon Volker Seitz has suggested, what is now urgently required is an independent supervisory body charged with assessing the efficacy of development policy initiatives – an international 'audit office' for development aid, whose remit year on year would be to carefully scrutinise how public bodies spend taxpayers' money.[222] After all, assistance for development is only meaningful if it actually fosters peoples' own initiative.

A Marshall Plan for Africa? Yes, but...

As misgivings continue to grow over the way aid has been delivered in the past, others are calling for a 'Marshall Plan for Africa' to promote the continent's ongoing development. I, too, have been advocating such a thing for many years. On his trip to Senegal, Niger and Rwanda in August 2016, Germany's minister for economic cooperation and development Gerd Müller added his voice to those in favour of this solution: 'We need to get away from the whole business of small-scale projects, from the development aid policies of past decades and adopt a totally new approach,' he announced.[223] In January 2017 the ministry published a policy document, titled *Cornerstones of a Marshall Plan for Africa*, in which it stated: 'We now need a new pact for future dealings between Europe and Africa.'

Everyone knows that enormous efforts will be required to advance the vast continent of Africa economically. This is particularly the case where the lack of infrastructure is concerned. For the most part, the transport routes that were inherited from the colonial rulers run only to the ports. Road and rail networks in the interior of individual countries are extremely inadequate, and links to neighbouring countries often only exist to a very rudimentary extent. Africa has no continent-wide network of air routes of the sort that we are familiar with in Europe; only Ethiopian Airlines links the east with the west and south of Africa. A 'big push' of the kind demanded by the economist Paul Collier as far back as 2006 could at last produce a significant advance for the continent.[224]

After the end of the Second World War, George Marshall, then the US secretary of state, devised his eponymous plan with the intention to help rebuild Europe. Between 1948 and 1952, this plan saw 16 European nations receive some $12.4 billion in the form of direct grants or loans. This equates to a sum of around $120 billion today. History has shown that the Marshall Plan was highly successful – even though the motives behind it were far from disinterested. The grants were only approved on the condition that they were used to purchase American goods. This initiative also transformed Europe into a consumer market for American companies. A Marshall Plan along these lines for Africa would undoubtedly do the continent more harm than good in the mid-term future.

However, the key question is: with whom might such a Marshall Plan for Africa be agreed? What could prevent all the money from ending up once more in the pockets of African autocrats who would use it to consolidate their grip on power? After all, there has been no shortage of grandiose plans and initiatives in the past. Taking the sum total of all the development aid that has been pumped into the continent as a basis, the Marshall Plan for Africa has long since been a reality. For example, the funding volume provided to Germany by the 1948 Marshall Plan amounted to around 2.5 per cent of the country's GDP at the time, which had been severely reduced by the effects of the war. Yet, even in the 1990s, sub-Saharan Africa received development aid that amounted to more than 12 per cent of its GDP.[225] If one wanted to ensure that the funding would reach its intended targets, some fundamental requirements would first have to be met. An international controlling body would be essential, such as that which every large firm possesses in the shape of a supervisory board. The African Union, the UN Economic Commission for Africa (UNECA) and the World Bank should be represented on it, and the release of funds should be monitored according to strict criteria. The most important criterion of all must be good governance.

'A country cannot be developed from the outside,' Deaton has said regarding development aid. 'Countries develop internally, and to do this they require a government and a population who are working together towards the same development goals.'[226] This would be the principal task facing European governments: they need to understand that economic development cannot be achieved without political development – in Africa, too. Europe finally has to put an end to the disastrous policy of appeasement towards African dictators. It is essential to note at this point that this is not a question of making prescriptive demands on how those in power should govern their country, nor of attempting to foist the state model of Western democracies on them. But one should nonetheless require that they at least observe the principles that African states have themselves recognised as binding. They are all signatories to the founding Charter of the UN and have committed themselves to observing human rights and the principle of the rule of law. Anyone in Africa who is not prepared to abide by these principles should have their support rescinded. The sovereign states of Africa have now been independent for more than 50 years. They quite rightly expect the West to treat them as equal partners. But an intrinsic part of such a relationship is being open to criticism as well. Governments that flout the principle of the rule of law and ride roughshod over human rights do not deserve any assistance.

And yet – to cite an oft-stated objection – if Europe were

to adopt this approach, wouldn't it lose its influence over its neighbouring continent? Would it not simply drive Africa straight into the arms of China, which does not make its support and economic cooperation contingent upon political demands, and which hallows above all the principle of non-interference in other countries' internal affairs? I see this as a specious argument, for most Africans have long since realised that China is pursuing its own agenda in Africa. They have not failed to notice that Beijing is primarily out to exploit Africa's mineral resources, which it requires to develop its own industrial base, and that it is has no interest in sustainability. In the words of the South African journalist Stanley Uys, the Chinese comport themselves in Africa 'like goats: after staying in a country for the required period, extracting the minerals they want, their legacy is – scrub, rocks and sand'.[227] Or, as it was put by the financier and former governor of the Nigerian Central Bank Lamido Sanusi, writing in the *Financial Times*: 'So China takes our primary goods and sells us manufactured ones. This was also the essence of colonialism.'[228] Many of the wholehearted proclamations and pledges made by China to invest in Africa's infrastructure have never been implemented, and the cheap consumer goods with which China has flooded the African market have permanently damaged its reputation among African consumers: television sets that give up the ghost after the first power cut; mobile phones whose batteries last barely a few weeks; T-shirts that fall apart the first time they are washed; and condoms that burst. In Zimbabwe, there is even a dedicated word for substandard, cheap goods from China: *zhing-zhong*.[229]

But is the West really so different to China in the way it behaves? Especially where textiles and agricultural produce are concerned, African producers are largely excluded from the markets of the EU and America. As a result of the agricultural protectionism practised by the Americans, Europeans and Japanese, it has been estimated that Africa loses around $30 billion in export revenue annually – fully half of the sum in development aid that flows into the continent every year. The industrialised countries of the West are vocal in their championing of the ideals of democracy, human rights and combatting corruption. But in the final analysis, it is clear that they only pay lip service to these principles. For the West's own strategic or economic interest it is all too willing to put such noble objectives on the back burner. Nevertheless, Africa's dictators clearly do understand plain speaking. I am convinced that a credible threat to choke off the supply of money to them would achieve the desired result.

Provided, that is, that Europe speaks with a single voice. As long as each country in the EU pursues its individual interests in Africa, Africa's leaders will continue to be able to play one off against the other. But if the EU were finally to bring itself to adopt a common policy, its word would carry far more weight. When will the EU finally link its provision of development aid to Africa to the strict condition that good governance be implemented – and in cases of doubt be prepared to draw the appropriate conclusion and halt its aid? The power of Africa's dictators only remains as entrenched as it is because they are, in Roosevelt's memorable phrasing, 'our bastards' – the 'bastards' of the West.

Truly effective aid for Africa

In all discussions about how best to help Africa, one factor must be clearly borne in mind: the best development aid comes in the form of good economic relations – provided these are conducted on an equal footing. It would be a good start if the UK and the other nations of Europe were to provide better securities and guarantees to their companies that wish to invest in Africa. Beijing offers every Chinese firm investing at least $1 million in Africa a 100 per cent state guarantee – thus furnishing Chinese enterprises with a significant locational advantage.

If Africa is to have a future, Europe must first and foremost abandon its catastrophic economic and trade policies. It must finally put an end to subsidising its farming industry at the cost of developing nations. It must urgently lobby for effective international sanctions to be put in place to combat the worldwide practice of land grabbing, which has robbed the poorest countries on Earth of their most precious asset – their agriculturally viable land. Notwithstanding all the necessary endeavours to bring industrialisation, farming is the real key to development on the African continent. Through improved methods of cultivation and measures against soil erosion, the crop yields in many African countries could be doubled without a great deal of effort. Africa requires broad-based support for small- and medium-scale farming – through micro-credits extended to local processing firms; through a programme of road building to give goods easer access to markets; and through halting the import of produce dumped on the market by European concerns, which effectively leave local producers high and dry. Africa needs aid for development that is sustainable and places a premium on individual initiative. Support for small entrepreneurs by means of micro-loans plays a central role in this, for even small sums are often enough to enable people to develop their own income sources and so to lift themselves up out of the poverty trap.

Above all, it is essential to help and encourage women, who represent the key to Africa's future. In the repayment of small personal loans, they are far more reliable than men; they tend not to spend their money on drink and they are less prone to corruption. In the areas of healthcare and education, their role is especially crucial: whenever mothers' levels of education increase, the incidence of infant and child mortality falls. And the longer girls go to school, the fewer children they conceive later in life. If Africa is to take its problem of population development firmly in hand, then it must invest in women.

Primarily, Europe must do all it can to ensure that Africa is properly governed. The same thing that applies to every country in the world of necessity also applies to the states of Africa: they can only develop if they are blessed with good governance. The exasperation of the young people of Africa with their autocratic rulers was indicated by the example of John Magufuli. Magufuli was elected as Tanzania's new president in the autumn of 2015. On taking office, he immediately announced that there would be a decisive push to combat corruption, nepotism and the squandering of tax revenues – promises that are often made by African leaders. But he set about matching his words with actions, calling off the planned celebrations to mark Tanzania's independence day on 9 December and cancelling the lavish state banquet for the opening of parliament. The money thereby saved, he declared, would instead be invested in increasing the number of hospital beds and in fighting cholera. After only a few weeks in power, Magufuli dismissed the board of the Tanzania Ports Authority and numerous leading civil servants, and pressed charges of corruption and maladministration against them. He also set up a task force to combat tax fraud. He slashed the bloated cabinet of his predecessor by half, to just 19 ministers, and capped their extortionate salaries. In addition, he abolished many of the privileges that ministers and top civil servants had previously enjoyed. For instance, they are no longer allowed to fly first class on trips abroad. The increased state revenue raised by these measures is to be used mainly for the improvement of education: as of the start of 2016, education in Tanzania from primary school through to high school matriculation is entirely free of charge.[230]

The policies enacted by Magufuli unleashed a storm of enthusiasm on social network sites across the whole of Africa. The continent's youth hailed the Tanzanian president as a new hero, and time and again one heard the phrase 'the new Mandela'. A new English verb began to do the rounds: 'to magufulify', meaning to sweep away corruption. And the most frequently asked question among Facebook, Twitter and countless blogs was: 'What would Magufuli do?'[231] The Tanzanian head of state still has to prove whether he can truly meet popular expectations and that, as president, he will abide by the democratic rules. In his chosen course of action, he will have to overcome endemic corruption within his own ruling party, which has governed Tanzania without interruption since independence. Moreover, most of his political counterparts on the continent regard him as a troublemaker and someone who is fouling his own nest. Yet Magufuli's example demonstrates once again how great the hunger for change is among the young people of Africa.

One thing is certain: no one from outside – not America, not Europe and not China either – will be able to 'save' Africa. Only Africa itself can do that, provided its people can regain their confidence and believe in their own strength. Only then will the exodus of talent from Africa come to an end. Africans must take their fate into their own hands – and Europe can and must help them to do so, such that the African continent, which is currently haemorrhaging its lifeblood, may become a continent with a future.

EPILOGUE

Martin Luther King Jr. famously had a dream that his children might one day live in a nation 'where they will not be judged by the colour of their skin, but by the content of their character'. He had a dream that his country the United States would be transformed into 'an oasis of freedom and justice'. King's dream may not have come to full fruition; the world today as a whole, let alone the United States, could scarcely be called 'an oasis of freedom and justice'. Yet the 54 years that have passed since King delivered his renowned speech have undoubtedly seen much change all the same. The situations in the world in which a person is judged by the colour of his or her skin have become fewer.

But when I think of Africa today, I am haunted by a recurrent nightmare. What would happen if it came to pass that millions of Africans, driven by despair and hopelessness, suddenly 'upped sticks' and turned their backs on their home continent? What would happen if they all came knocking at the gates of Europe? How would Europe stop them? Would they be deterred by walls and barbed wire, and ranks of police officers and soldiers? Which head of government would want to take on the responsibility of giving the order to fire on peaceful, unarmed civilians who want nothing more than to find a safe haven? And what would happen to the police and soldiers who were given such an order? What would be the devastating traumatic psychological effects on them of carrying it out?

How long would it be before they disobeyed and laid down their weapons?

Let us fervently hope that it never comes to this. Europe and the other industrialised nations of the West must finally set about tackling the root causes of flight and displacement. This urgent task has been put off for far too long. It is not just Africa's but all of our futures that are at stake here. Does Europe intend to keep standing idly by, shrugging its shoulders and watching thousands of people, who see the continent as their lifeline, die a miserable death by drowning off its coasts? The people who have taken on the huge risk of a perilous sea crossing still believe in Europe. But do Europeans themselves? Confronted by the refugees seeking to gain entry, will Europe abandon all the ideals and principles that make it what it is – its humanity, its shared values? In giving up on Africa, will Europe also give up on itself?

In the debate that has raged in Europe about what policy to adopt towards refugees, one frequently hears the sentiment that the migration crisis has divided Europe. But it is not the people who are seeking shelter and asylum in Europe who have divided the continent. It is the governments of Europe that have done this themselves, by recanting on the principle of solidarity with one another. For far too long now, Europe has left the states on its periphery, along with the refugees who mass at these borders, to their own devices.

For centuries the nations of Europe were locked in wars. The last two major conflicts, which in the twentieth century spread to become world wars, devastated the continent like never before in human history. From the ashes of the Second World War there arose a loose confederation of countries that would eventually grow to become the present EU. Its formation was based on the recognition that the citizens of Europe would only be able to enjoy a life of peace and freedom through common endeavour and cooperation. Just over 70 years after the end of the war, Europe once again finds itself at risk of disintegrating into insular nation-states and petty rivalries. Have Europe's governments learnt nothing from history? Does Europe still believe in itself? Does it still have faith in a shared future?

In late November 2017, a large group of African and European leaders met in Abidjan, the capital of Côte d'Ivoire, for the fifth African Union – European Union Summit. The keynote motto for the conference was 'Investing in Youth for a Sustainable Future'. As so often on such occasions, the summit's closing declaration was full of fine words about future cooperation between the neighbouring continents. Not for the first time, a 'global partnership' was proposed, while 'investment in education and technology', 'greater political stability and security' and a 'lasting structural change in Africa' were all identified as necessary goals. Yet the conference was largely silent on the question of how all these things were to be brought about.

African heads of state cut increasingly confident figures at such meetings. They see themselves as the great consumer market of the future. It seems self-evident to Africans that European industry will want to invest in Africa, especially since China, Turkey, Qatar and many other states are queuing up to trade with the continent. At a joint press conference during French president Emmanuel Macron's state visit to Ghana immediately after the summit, his Ghanaian counterpart President Nana Addo Dankwa Akufo-Addo clearly expressed the prevailing mood: 'We can no longer pursue a policy for our countries and regions that is based on the support given by the West, France or the European Union. This has not worked and it will not work [...] It is not right for a country like Ghana – 60 years after its independence – to depend on the generosity of European taxpayers when it comes to financial means for health or education.' Ghana Beyond Aid is the banner headline of the policy being pursued by the administration of the Ghanaian president, who came to power in January 2017. In other words, it represents a move away by African states from dependency on development aid to taking responsibility for themselves. To achieve this, the government of Ghana intends to use political means to stimulate economic growth and to modernise agriculture. Yet this will not be achieved without some foreign investment – namely from Europe, which is Ghana's largest trading partner.

Mobile phone images taken just before the conference and published by the US broadcaster CNN vividly demonstrate what life looks like at present for Africa's young people. These showed young black Africans being mistreated and enslaved in Libya. They were being auctioned for a few hundred Libyan dinars per person at a slave market. Across that country, up to a million men, women and children are currently thought to be held in overcrowded internment camps. These are being de facto run by the Libyans on behalf of the EU, as a way of preventing refugees from attempting the sea crossing to Europe.

Unlike Germany, France, Italy and most other EU member states, the UK was only represented at the African Union – European Union Summit by a secretary of state. Since 29 March 2017, when the British prime minister, Theresa May, officially submitted written notification to the European Council of the UK's intention to leave the EU in spring 2019, tough negotiations about 'Brexit' have been ongoing. Yet, even if the UK does end up leaving the EU, it will still be imperative to have common European foreign and security policies – also, and particularly so, with regard to Africa. The UK formerly played a key role in the abolition of the slave trade in Africa and worldwide, and it is inconceivable that it would be willing to stand idly by and witness a renaissance of people-trafficking on the neighbouring continent.

Europe will not be able to isolate itself without losing face. It must mount a stout defence of its principles and aims – both in the face of those countries in its midst which no longer take these ideals seriously and with regard to Africa. Europe must realise that a common future, underpinned by democratic principles and a fair system of global trade, is the only way forward. In the process, Europe must be prepared to give up a little of its prosperity. But no one should be fearful of such a prospect – quite the contrary. If we, Africans and Europeans, stand together and meet the challenges that face us with courage and confidence, the future will be to our great mutual benefit – culturally, in human terms and, not least, economically. The only way we can achieve this common goal is if European politicians have the courage to make good governance in Africa the sine qua non of future Afro-European development cooperation.

NOTES

1   'Global Trends: Forced Displacement in 2015' [PDF], *UNHCR*, 20 June 2016, http://www.unhcr.org/statistics/unhcrstats/576408cd7/unhcr-global-trends-2015.html (accessed 1 August 2016).

2   Ibid, p. 5

3   'Global Migration Trends Factsheet', *International Organization for Migration*, Berlin, April 2016, http://gmdac.iom.int/global-migration-trends-factsheet (accessed 1 August 2016).

4   R. L. Stevenson, *From 'Emigrant aus Leidenschaft The Amateur Emigrant'*, Zürich, Manesse Verlag, 2005 by Robert Louis Stevenson (1895).

5   Cf. J. Oltmer, *Globale Migration: Geschichte und Gegenwart*, Munich, Verlag C.H. Beck, 2012, pp. 20f.

6   'The 1951 Convention relating to the Status of Refugees and its 1967 Protocol', *Rights in Exile Programme*, http://www.refugeelegalaidinformation.org/1951-convention (accessed 8 January 2018).

7   The statistics cited here and in the following pages on the numbers of refugees as of the end of 2015 are taken from: 'Global Trends: Forced Displacement in 2015', op. cit.

8   'Global Trends: Forced Displacement in 2015', op. cit., p. 14.

9   'Refugees from Somalia', *UNHCR*, 21 April 2016,
    http://data.unhcr.org/horn-of-africa/region.
    php?id=3&country=110.

10 B. Rawlence, *City of Thorns: Nine Lives in the World's
    Largest Refugee Camp*, London, Portobello Books, 2016.

11 '"We Want to Go Back Home" the cry of peace at
    Nyarugusu refugees camp' [online video], 2011, https://
    www.youtube.com/watch?v=vEqriZ4jOc8 (accessed 1
    August 2016).

12 Cf. Rawlence, op. cit.

13 A. Göbel, 'Armee-Offensive gegen Islamisten: Nigerias
    Kampf gegen Boko Haram', *Tagesschau.de*, 17 May 2013,
    http://www.webcitation.org/6GgWkH24L (accessed 22
    January 2018).

14 'Nigeria 2015/2016', *Amnesty International*, https://www.
    amnesty.org/en/countries/africa/nigeria/report-nigeria/
    (accessed 1 August 2016).

15 T. Cole, 'Migrants are welcome', *Verso Books* [web blog],
    7 September 2015, https://www.versobooks.com/
    blogs/2226-teju-cole-migrants-are-welcome (accessed 8
    January 2018).

16 'Die Flüchtlings-Industrie: Interview mit Ben Rawlence'
    [The Refugee Industry: Interview with Ben Rawlence],
    Süddeutsche Zeitung, 1 June 2016, p. 11.

17 'Risk Analysis for 2016' [PDF], *Frontex*, March 2016,
    http://frontex.europa.eu/assets/Publications/Risk_
    Analysis/Annula_Risk_Analysis_2016.pdf, p. 6 (accessed
    1 August 2016).

18 Ibid., p. 18.

19 The significance of this survey is undermined by the fact
    that Frontex was unable to ascertain the nationality of

those making irregular border crossings in fully 31 per cent of cases.

20 'Mediterranean death toll soars in first 5 months of 2016', *UNHCR*, 31 May 2016, http://www.unhcr.org/uk/news/ latest/2016/5/574db9d94/mediterranean-death-toll-soars-first-5-months-2016.html (accessed 9 January 2018).

21 Ibid.

22 'Vermutlich schon mehr als 3600 tote Flüchtlinge in diesem Jahr' [Probably more than 3,600 dead refugees this year], *Der Tagesspiegel*, 14 July 2017, http://www.tagesspiegel.de/politik/ migration-vermutlich-schon-mehr-als-3600-tote-fluechtlinge-in-diesem-jahr/13874358.html (accessed 1 August 2016).

23 L. Guelpa, 'Esodo biblico dal Kenya: "In 600mila verso l'Italia"', *Il Giornale*, 13 May 2016, http://www.ilgiornale. it/news/politica/esodo-biblico-kenya-600mila-verso-litalia-1257987.html (accessed 22 January 2018).

24 C. Ehrhardt, 'Banges Warten auf das Boot nach Europa', *Frankfurter Allgemeine Zeitung*, 3 August 2016, http://www.faz.net/aktuell/politik/ausland/afrika/ im-libyschen-misrata-warten-migranten-auf-das-boot-nach-europa-14367324.html.

25 N. Farah, 'Europa und Afrika', *Du: Zeitschrift der Kulturen*, no. 656, December 1995/January 1996, p. 12.

26 A. Selle, 'Drei Erden für die Menschheit', *Der Tagesspiegel*, 11 July 2016.

27 R. Kipling, 'Boots: Infantry Columns', *Poetry Lovers' Page*, http://www.poetryloverspage.com/poets/kipling/ boots.html (accessed 1 July 2016).

28 'Luba Caryatid Stool Achieves Record for a Work of African Art at Sotheby's: $7.1 Million'

ArtDaily, http://artdaily.com/news/43060/
Luba-Caryatid-Stool-Achieves-Record-for-a-Work-of-
African-Art-at-Sotheby-s---7-1-Million#.WlYnGZOFiu5
(accessed 10 January 2018).

29   L. van Dijk, *Die Geschichte Afrikas*, Frankfurt am Main,
Campus Verlag, 2004, p. 84.

30   Cf. D. Eltis and D. Richardson, *Extending the Frontiers*,
New Haven, Yale University Press, 2008.

31   D. Van Reybrouck, *Congo: The Epic History of a People*,
London, Ecco Press, 2015.

32   Cf. G. Graichen, H. Gründer, and H. Diedrich,
Deutsche Kolonien: Traum und Trauma, Berlin, Ullstein
Buchverlage, 2015, pp. 93–97.

33   The document containing von Trotha's notorious
'extermination order' can be found in the German
Federal Archives (Bundesarchiv) in Koblenz, under the
reference R 1001/2089.

34   In recent years, doubts have been raised about the
extent of the German crimes against the Herero and
the number of those killed. See M. Brehl, 'Diese
Schwarzen haben vor Gott und Menschen den Tod
verdient. Der Völkermord an den Herero 1904 und seine
zeitgenössische Legitimation', in I. Wojak and S. Meinl
(eds.), *Völkermord und Kriegsverbrechen in der ersten
Hälfte des 20. Jahrhunderts*, Frankfurt am Main, Campus
Verlag, 2004; and B. Grill, 'Gewisse Ungewissheiten', *Der
Spiegel*, no. 24, 2016, pp. 54–59.

35   van Dijk, op. cit., pp. 110f.

36   M. Baer and O. Schröter, *Eine Kopfjagd. Deutsche in
Ostafrika. Spuren kolonialer Herrschaft*, Berlin, Ch. Links
Verlag, 2001.

37 See M. Crowder, 'Indirect Rule: French and British Style', *Africa: Journal of the International African Institute*, vol. 34, no. 3, 1964, pp. 197–205.

38 Cf. A. Hochschild, *King Leopold's Ghost: A Story of Greed, Terror and Heroism in Colonial Africa*, London, Mariner Books, 1999.

39 J. Conrad, *Heart of Darkness,* http://www.gutenberg. org/ebooks/526 (accessed 10 January 2018).

40 Kipling's poem coined the phrase 'east of Suez', which became a key concept in British journalism and foreign policy.

41 The uprising was named for the supposedly miraculous waters known as Maji Maji (*maji* is the Swahili word for 'water'). This mixture of water, maize and sorghum seeds, which the warriors either drank or rubbed on their skin, was reputed to have magical powers. It allegedly rendered a person invulnerable and capable of shrugging off, like raindrops, the bullets fired by enemy soldiers.

42 G. Knopp, *Das Weltreich der Deutschen*, Munich, Pendo, 2011, p. 271.

43 F. Ansprenger, *Politische Geschichte Afrikas im 20. Jahrhundert*, Munich, C.H. Beck, 1999, p. 18.

44 van Dijk, op. cit., p. 115.

45 Ansprenger, op. cit., pp. 31f.

46 Graichen, Gründer, and Diedrich, op. cit., p. 374.

47 H. Krieger (ed.), *Die Welt seit 1945, Teil 1: Materialien für den Geschichtsunterricht*, Frankfurt am Main, Diesterweg, 1983, p. 1.

48 van Dijk, op. cit., p. 118f.

49 Cf. H. Sasse, *Die asiatisch-afrikanischen Staaten auf der Bandung-Konferenz*, Frankfurt am Main, Metzner, 1958.

50 Van Reybrouck, op. cit.

51 On the role played by Belgium in the plot to oust Patrice Lumumba, see L. de Witte, *Regierungsauftrag Mord: Der Tod Lumumbas und die Kongo-Krise*, Leipzig, Forum Vlg Leipzig, 2001.

52 See M. Baer and A. Böhm, 'Raketen für Afrika', *Die Zeit*, no. 32, 31 July 2008.

53 F. Fanon, *Peau noire, masques blancs*, Paris, Éditions du Seuil, 1952.

54 'Eritrea and Ethiopia: The Human Rights Agenda', *Amnesty International*, http://www.amnesty.org/en/ documents/AFR25/009/1991/en/ (accessed 11 July 2016).

55 Cf. P. Keatly, 'Obituary: Idi Amin', *The Guardian*, 18 August 2003.

56 S. Koelbl and J. Puhl, 'Richtet euch doch selbst', *Der Spiegel*, no. 24, 11 June 2016, p. 98f.

57 'In Uganda droht Homosexuellen lebenslange Haft' [Homosexuals in Uganda Threatened with Life Imprisonment], *Zeit-Online*, 24 February 2014, http:// www.zeit.de/politik/ausland/2014-02/uganda-museveni-homosexualitaet (accessed 10 July 2016).

58 B. Grill, *Ach, Afrika: Berichte aus dem Inneren eines Kontinents*, Munich, Goldmann Verlag, 2005, pp. 72f.

59 A. Perry, *In Afrika. Reise in die Zukunft*, Frankfurt am Main, S. Fischer, 2016, p. 178.

60 Ibid.

61 'Zimbabwe to sell $1.7bn diamond stockpile', *Financial Times*, 1 July 2010, https://www.ft.com/content/ 75c84f96-845d-11df-9cbb-00144feabdc0. For the document published by Wikileaks, see 'Regime elites looting deadly diamond field', *Wikileaks*, https://web. archive.org/web/20101212233003if_/http://213.251.145.

96:80/cable/2008/11/08HARARE1016.html#help_1 (accessed 11 July 2016).

62   Perry, op. cit., p. 246.

63   A. Césaire, *Discourse on Colonialism*, trans. Joan Pinkham, New York and London, Monthly Review Press, 1972.

64   See 'Bundesregierung nennt Herero-Massaker erstmals "Völkermord"', *Der Spiegel*, 10 July 2015, http://www.spiegel.de/politik/deutschland/namibia-massaker-bundesregierung-spricht-von-voelkermord-a-1043117.html (accessed 11 July 2016).

65   'Guerre d'Algérie et combats en Tunisie et au Maroc', *Sénat*, http://www.senat.fr/dossier-legislatif/ppl98-418.html (accessed 10 July 2016).

66   S. Bohland, 'Eine Frau glaubt an Afrika', *ARD-Weltspiegel*, 5 June 2016, http://www.daserste.de/information/politik-weltgeschehen/weltspiegel/nigeria-128.html (accessed 15 January 2018).

67   'Lions on the move: The progress and potential of African economies', *McKinsey Global Institute*, June 2010, http://www.mckinsey.com/global-themes/middle-east-and-africa/lions-on-the-move (accessed 15 January 2018).

68   Cf. 'Tax us if you can: Why Africa should stand up for Tax Justice' [PDF], *Tax Justice Network-Africa*, January 2011, https://www.taxjustice.net/cms/upload/pdf/tuiyc_africa_final.pdf (accessed 15 January 2018).

69   '2016 Cost of Living Ranking', *Mercer*, 22 June 2016, https://www.imercer.com/content/2016-cost-of-living-infographic.aspx (accessed 30 July 2016).

70   A. Sieren and F. Sieren, *Der Afrika-Boom: Die große Überraschung des 21. Jahrhunderts*, Munich, Carl Hanser Verlag, 2015, p. 230.

71 According to prognoses given by the World Bank and the
    International Monetary Fund in summer 2016.

72 A. Leke and D. Barton, '3 reasons things are looking up
    for African economies', *World Economic Forum*, 5 May
    2016, https://www.weforum.org/agenda/2016/05/what-
    s-the-future-of-economic-growth-in-africa/ (accessed 1
    August 2016).

73 'The 1.2 Billion Opportunity', *The Economist*, 16 April
    2016.

74 C. Hesse and S.G. Jánszky, 'Afrika 2025: Trendstudie
    des 2b AHEAD ThinkTanks' [PDF], *Afrika-Verein
    der deutschen Wirtschaft*, 5 June 2014, http://www.
    afrikaverein.de/uploads/media/Trendstudie_AV_-_
    Afrika_2025.pdf (accessed 20 July 2016).

75 Leke and Barton, op. cit.

76 Sieren and Sieren, op. cit., p. 25.

77 'Chinese Investment in Africa: Not as easy as it looks',
    The Economist, 21 November 2015, pp. 35f.

78 A. Wade, 'Time for the west to practise what it
    preaches', *The Financial Times*, 23 January 2008, http://
    www.ft.com/cms/s/0/5d347f88-c897-11dc-94a6-
    0000779fd2ac.html (accessed 1 July 2016).

79 'China steckt 46 Milliarden Dollar in Afrikas
    Wirtschaft', *China Internet Information Center*, 31 July
    2016, http://german.china.org.cn/txt/2016-07/31/
    content_38992644.htm (accessed 1 August 2016).

80 Deutsche Bundesbank and Afrika-Verein der deutschen
    Wirtschaft, personal communication, April 2016.

81 B. Grill, 'Afrikas Aufschwung XL', *Die Zeit*, no. 49,
    2 December 2010. http://www.zeit.de/2010/49/
    Aufschwung-Afrika (accessed 1 July 2016).

82 J. Manyika et al., 'Lions go digital: The Internet's transformative potential in Africa', *McKinsey Global Institute*, November 2013. http://www.mckinsey.com/ industries/high-tech/our-insights/lions-go-digital-the-internets-transformative-potential-in-africa

83 A. Bengelstorff, 'A Global Success from Kenya', *Credit Suisse*, 6 August 2015, https://www.credit-suisse.com/ ch/en/news-and-expertise/banking/articles/news-and-expertise/2015/08/en/a-global-success-from-kenya.html (accessed 1 July 2016).

84 S. Faris, 'The Solar Company Making a Profit on Poor Africans', *Bloomberg Businessweek*, 2 December 2015. http://www.bloomberg.com/features/2015-mkopa-solar-in-africa (accessed 1 July 2016).

85 'Virtual headaches: E-commerce firms Like Jumia have to beat multiple handicaps', *The Economist: Business in Africa*, 16 April 2016, p. 14.

86 'The middle class: A matter of definition', *The Economist: Business in Africa*, 16 April 2016, pp. 5f.

87 R. Dowden, 'Africa's Illusive Middle Class', *Royal African Society*, 4 January 2016, http://www.royalafricansociety. org/blog/africa%E2%80%99s-illusive-middle-class (accessed 1 July 2016).

88 Grill, 'Afrikas Aufschwung XL', op. cit.

89 The Fragile States Index is based on 12 indicators: demographic pressures (high volume population density); refugees and internally displaced persons; 'group grievance' (the existence of tension between groups); human flight and brain drain; uneven economic development and group-based inequality; poverty and economic decline; increasing corruption and decline of state legitimacy; disappearance of basic

state functions and services; human rights violations; a security apparatus acting with impunity; the emergence of factionalised elites; and external intervention. See 'Fragile States Index 2016' [PDF], *The Fund for Peace*, 27 June 2016, http://library.fundforpeace.org/fsi16-report (accessed 1 July 2016).

90 G. Mills, *Why Africa is Poor: And What Africans Can Do About It*, Johannesburg, Penguin Books (South Africa), 2010.

91 'Der neue Wachstumsstar in Afrika', *Handelsblatt*, 21 November 2015.

92 'World Economic Outlook Database', *International Monetary Fund*, April 2016, https://www.imf.org/external/pubs/ft/weo/2016/01/weodata/index.aspx (accessed 1 July 2016).

93 C. Hecking, 'Strom wie Heu', *Die Zeit*, no. 28, 30 June 2016.

94 'Ethiopia's Grand Renaissance Dam 60 pct completed', *Xinhua*, 8 August 2017, http://news.xinhuanet.com/english/2017-08/08/c_136506781.htm (accessed 16 January 2018).

95 F. von Schönfeld, 'Hungersnot in Äthiopien', *Frankfurter Allgemeine Zeitung*, 13 May 2016.

96 'Report on recognition of agriculture as a strategic sector in the context of food security', *European Parliament*, 16 December 2010, http://www.europarl.europa.eu/sides/getDoc.do?pubRef=-//EP//TEXT+REPORT+A7-2010-0376+0+DOC+XML+V0//EN&language=hr (accessed 16 January 2018). On world hunger, see also: M. Caparrós, *Der Hunger*, trans. S. Giersberg and H. Grzimek, Berlin, Suhrkamp Verlag, 2015; M. Brüntrup,

'Welthunger und Welternährung', *Aus Politik und Zeitgeschichte*, no. 49, 2015, pp. 6–13.

97 'The State of Food Security and Nutrition in the World 2017' [PDF], *Food and Agriculture Organization of the United Nations*, 2017, http://www.fao.org/3/a-I7695e.pdf (accessed 20 July 2016).

98 'Welthunger-Index 2017' [PDF], *Welthungerhilfe*, October 2017, https://www.welthungerhilfe.de/fileadmin/user_upload/Themen/Welthungerindex/WHI_2017/Welthungerindex_2017.pdf (accessed 16 January 2018).

99 Caparrós, op. cit., p. 22.

100 Cf. Perry, op. cit., pp. 29–43.

101 'Welthunger-Index 2015: Krieg und Hunger', *Weltthungerhilfe*, 12 October 2015, https://www.welthungerhilfe.de/welthungerindex2015 (accessed 26 July 2016), p. 17.

102 C. Mayer, 'This asset is like gold, only better', *Daily Wealth*, 4 October 2009, http://www.stockhouse.com/opinion/independent-reports/2009/10/04/this-asset-is-like-gold,-only-better (accessed 16 January 2018).

103 Major development research organisations are involved in compiling the Land Matrix database, including the International Land Coalition (a coalition of institutions such as the World Bank and the UN) and various NGOs. See *Land Matrix Global Observatory*, http://www.landmatrix.org (accessed 1 August 2016).

104 J. Baxter, 'Wie Gold, nur besser: Fette Dividenden aus Afrikas Böden', *Le Monde Diplomatique*, 15 January 2010, https://monde-diplomatique.de/artikel/!502760 (accessed 16 January 2018).

105 Information correct as of July 2016. The remaining land was earmarked for several crops simultaneously. See 'Agricultural Drivers', *Land Matrix Global Observatory*, http://www.landmatrix.org/en/get-the-idea/ agricultural-drivers (accessed 1 August 2016).

106 W. Bommert, 'Fass ohne Boden. Der Handel mit Land wird zum weltweiten Geschäft', *FROH! Magazin*, no. 10, 2013, pp. 80–86.

107 'Fruchtbarer Boden für Schnittblumen', *Die Tageszeitung*, 16 November 2011.

108 'Der neue Wachstumsstar in Afrika', op. cit.

109 L. Cotula, *The Great African Land Grab?: Agricultural Investments and the Global Food System*, London, Zed Books, 2013, pp. 100f.

110 I. Michler and E.A. Ginten, 'Rücksichtslose Jagd auf den neuen, alten Bodenschatz', *Die Welt*, 19 January 2016, http://www.welt.de/wirtschaft/article151170043/ Ruecksichtslose-Jagd-auf-den-neuen-alten-Bodenschatz. html (accessed 1 August 2016).

111 'The debate over big land data', *The Financial Times*, 1 March 2016, https://www.ft.com/content/ df31f666-0a43-3a0e-a747-ec72f2efb40c.

112 M. Tran, 'Land Deals in Africa have led to a Wild West – bring on the sheriff, says FAO', *The Guardian*, 29 October 2012, https://www.theguardian.com/ global-development/2012/oct/29/land-deals-africa-wild-west-fao (accessed 1 August 2016).

113 'Voluntary Guidelines on the Responsible Governance of Tenure of Land, Fisheries and Forests in the Context of National Food Security', *Food and Agriculture Organization of the United Nations*, 2012, http://www.

fao.org/docrep/016/i2801e/i2801e.pdf (accessed 1
August 2016).

114 'Soziale und demografische Daten weltweit: DSW-
Datenreport 2017', *Deutsche Stiftung Weltbevölkerung*,
August 2017, https://www.dsw.org/wp-content/
uploads/2017/08/DSW-Datenreport_2017_web.pdf
(accessed 16 January 2018).

115 'The World Factbook 2015', *Central Intelligence Agency*,
https://www.cia.gov/library/publications/the-world-
factbook (accessed 1 July 2016).

116 'Datenreport 2015', *Deutsche Stiftung Weltbevölkerung*,
August 2015, https://www.yumpu.com/en/
document/view/53248755/datenreport-2015-stiftung-
weltbevoelkerungpdf (accessed 16 January 2018), p. 4.

117 Intergovernmental Panel on Climate Change, *Climate
Change 2014 – Impacts, Adaptation and Vulnerability*,
Cambridge, Cambridge University Press, 2014.

118 See A. Sinai, 'Verwüstung: Wie der Klimawandel
Konflikte anheizt', *Le Monde Diplomatique*, 10
September 2015.

119 G. Dyer, *Climate Wars: The Fight for Survival as the
World Overheats*, London, Scribe Publications, 2008.

120 N. Shaxson, *Poisoned Wells: The Dirty Politics of African
Oil*, London, Palgrave Macmillan, 2008, p. 4.

121 Perry, op. cit., p. 335.

122 K. Maier, *This House Has Fallen: Midnight in Nigeria*,
New York, Basic Books, 2003.

123: 'Eine gute Zeit für Nigeria', *Afrika-Verein der deutschen
Wirtschaft*, October 2015, http://www.afrikaverein.de/
uploads/media/Hintergrundpapier_AV_-_Nigeria.pdf
(accessed 15 July 2016).

124 C. Braeckman, 'Der Katanga-Boom: Kupfer und Kobalt locken Investoren in den Süden des Kongo', *Le Monde Diplomatique*, no. 5, pp. 67–75.

125 Van Reybrouck, op. cit., p. 621.

126 M. Jullien, 'Katanga: Fighting for DR Congo's cash cow to secede', *BBC News*, 12 August 2013, http://www.bbc.com/news/world-africa-23422038 (accessed 1 August 2016).

127 A. Ross, 'Protest, tear gas in Congo as Sassou Nguesso seeks to extend rule', *Reuters*, 20 March 2016, http://www.reuters.com/article/us-congo-election-idUSKCN0WM0B2 (accessed 15 July 2016).

128 T. Zick and J. Tilouine, 'Unter Kleptokraten', *Süddeutsche Zeitung*, 14 April 2016.

129 F. Müller-Jung and A.B. Jalloh, 'Panama Papers: Diese Afrikaner stehen unter Druck', *Deutsche Welle*, 5 April 2016. http://dw.com/p/1IPJN (accessed 28 July 2016).

130 Wolfgang Tuck, 'Neue Fälle: Wie Offshore-Firmen dabei helfen, Afrika auszuplündern', *WirtschaftsBlatt*, 26 July 2016.

131 T. Zick, 'Kopflos', *Süddeutsche Zeitung*, 22/23 August 2015.

132 Müller-Jung and Jahlloh, op. cit.

133 Corruption Perceptions Index 2015, *Transparency International*, http://www.transparency.org/cpi2015 (accessed 1 August 2016).

134 *Mo Ibrahim Foundation*, http://mo.ibrahim.foundation (accessed 1 August 2016).

135 'Ibrahim Index of African Governance', *Mo Ibrahim Foundation*, http://mo.ibrahim.foundation/iiag/data-portal (accessed 1 August 2016).

136 M. Cohen and S. Butera, 'Africa's Would-Be Switzerland Shows Economic Clout with WEF', *Bloomberg*, 10 May 2016, http://www.bloomberg.com/news/articles/2016-05-09/africa-s-would-be-switzerland-flaunts-economic-prowess-with-wef (accessed 15 July 2016).

137 J. Johannsen, 'Referendum in Ruanda: Kagames Anhänger üben Druck auf die Bevölkerung aus', *Deutschlandfunk Kultur*, 18 December 2015.

138 W. Drechsler, 'Kontinent der Extreme', *Der Tagesspiegel*, 3 January 2016, http://www.tagesspiegel.de/politik/25-jahre-afrika-korrespondent-kontinent-der-extreme/12783294.html (accessed 15 July 2016).

139 M. Yonas and B. Morgenrath, 'Äthiopien: Oromo-Proteste gegen Landraub', *Deutsche Welle*, 25 December 2015, http://dw.com/p/1HPQB (accessed 30 July 2016).

140 'Äthiopien: Entfesselter Volkszorn', *Der Spiegel*, no. 33, 13 August 2016.

141 D. Dehmer, 'Vereinte Nationen warnen vor Völkermord in Burundi', *Der Tagesspiegel*, 21 December 2015, http://www.tagesspiegel.de/politik/burundi-vor-neuem-buergerkrieg-vereinte-nationen-warnen-vor-voelkermord-in-burundi/12752548.html (accessed 30 July 2016).

142 'Burundi: Göttliches Mandat für den Präsidenten', *Frankfurter Allgemeine*, 24 July 2016, http://www.faz.net/aktuell/politik/ausland/afrika/burundischer-staatschef-nkurunziza-will-dritte-amtszeit-13719686.html (accessed 30 July 2016).

143 Cf. T. Monénembo, 'Nkurunziza und andere Potentaten', *Le Monde Diplomatique*, 10 December 2015.

144 Ibid.

145 P. Collier, *Wars, Guns, and Votes: Democracy in Dangerous Places*, London, Vintage, 2010.

146 D. Acemoglu and J. A. Robinson, *Why Nations Fail: The Origins of Power, Prosperity and Poverty*, London, Profile Books, 2013.

147 See U. Menzel, 'Der Zerfall der postkolonialen Staaten', *Aus Politik und Zeitgeschichte*, no.18/19, 2001, pp. 3–5.

148 M. Braun, 'Auf einen Blick: Afrikaner vor dem IStGH', *Deutsche Welle*, 21 June 2016, http://www.dw.com/de/auf-einen-blick-afrikaner-vor-dem-istgh/a-17410829 (accessed 1 August 2016).

149 S. Koelbl and J. Puhl, 'Richtet euch doch selbst', *Der Spiegel*, no. 24, 1 June 2016, pp. 98–100.

150 D. Pelz, 'AU auf dem Kriegspfad gegen den IStGH', *Deutsche Welle*, 18 July 2016, http://www.dw.com/de/au-auf-dem-kriegspfad-gegen-den-istgh/a-19408378 (accessed 1 August 2016).

151 D. Köpp, 'Habré-Urteil hoffentlich ein Präzedenzfall', *Deutsche Welle*, 30 May 2016, http://www.dw.com/de/kommentar-habr%C3%A9-urteil-hoffentlich-ein-pr%C3%A4zedenzfall/a-19294085 (accessed 1 August 2016). On the history of the indictment and trial of Hissène Habré, see B. Grill, 'Das Ende des Schweigens', *Der Spiegel*, no. 40, 26 September 2015, pp. 96–99.

152 D. Johnson 'Keine neue starke Frau für Afrika', *Die Tageszeitung*, 19 July 2016.

153 'Global Trends: Forced Displacement in 2015', op. cit., p. 17.

154 T. Lynch, 'The Country That's Never Had an Election', *Foreign Policy*, 6 November 2013, http://foreignpolicy.com/2013/11/06/the-country-thats-never-had-an-election (accessed 1 August 2016).

155 '2017 World Press Freedom Index', *Reporters Without Borders*, https://rsf.org/en/ranking (accessed 30 July 2016).

156 M. Freidel, 'Von wegen Freiheit', *Frankfurter Allgemeine*, 12 May 2016, http://www.faz.net/-gpf-8gsyl (accessed 1 August 2016).

157 N. Hirt, 'Flüchtlinge aus Eritrea: Spielball europäischer Interessen', *GIGA Focus Afrika*, no. 2, July 2016.

158 'Simbabwe: Wie Diktatur und Misswirtschaft Menschen ins Ausland treiben', *KAS-Auslandsinformationen*, no. 2/3, 2015, pp. 101–106.

159 H. Behrendt-Kigozi, 'Perspektive Westafrika: Migration und Brain-Drain in Nigeria', in *Flucht und Migration als Herausforderung für Europa* [PDF], Berlin, Konrad-Adenauer-Stiftung, 2016, http://www.kas.de/wf/ de/33.44316 (accessed 1 July 2016), pp. 98f.

160 'Global Trends: Forced Displacement in 2015', op. cit., p. 15.

161 N. Macheroux-Denault, 'Deutschlands Ruf dringt bis nach Mali', *Die Welt*, 13 October 2015.

162 Zick, 'Kopflos', op. cit.

163 I. Pfaff, 'Afrikas Regierende sorgen sich vor allem um einander, weniger um ihre Bürger', *Süddeutsche Zeitung*, 14 February 2016, http://www.sueddeutsche.de/politik/ muenchner-sicherheitskonferenz-afrikas-regierende-sorgen-sich-vor-allem-um-einander-weniger-um-ihre-buerger-1.2863156 (accessed 1 July 2016).

164 T. Hagmann 'Wie ich mich mit dem äthiopischen Regime anlegte', *NZZ am Sonntag*, 3 July 2016, pp. 52f.

165 'Historische Wahlschlappe für den ANC', *Deutsche Welle*, 6 August 2016, http://dw.com/p/1JcjS (accessed 8 August 2016).

166 S. Mbaye: 'Senegal – Mythen und Fakten', *Le Monde Diplomatique*, 10 February 2012.

167 'Senegal's President-elect Macky Sall hails "new era"', *BBC News*, 26 March 2012, http://www.bbc.co.uk/news/world-africa-17508098 (accessed 17 January 2018).

168 R. Alkousaa et al., 'Das Märchen eines Sommers', *Der Spiegel*, no. 33, 13 August 2016, pp. 20–28.

169 N. Fried, '… dann ist das nicht mein Land', *Süddeutsche Zeitung*, 15 September 2016, http://www.sueddeutsche.de/politik/merkel-zu-fluechtlingspolitik-dann-ist-das-nicht-mein-land-1.2648819 (accessed 1 August 2016).

170 'Frankreich lehnt EU-Flüchtlingskontingente ab', *Zeit-Online*, 13 February 2016, http://www.zeit.de/politik/ausland/2016-02/manuel-valls-fluechtlinge-frankreich-kontingente-angela-merkel (accessed 1 August 2016).

171 S. Mülherr, 'Es wird nicht ohne hässliche Bilder gehen', *Die Welt*, 13 January 2016, http://www.welt.de/politik/ausland/article150933461/Es-wird-nicht-ohne-haessliche-Bilder-gehen.html (accessed 1 August 2016).

172 'Österreichs Außenminister will Flüchtlinge auf Inseln internieren', *Zeit-Online*, 5 June 2016. http://www.zeit.de/politik/ausland/2016-06/fluechtlinge-oesterreich-sebastian-kurz-mittelmeer (accessed 1 July 2016).

173 B. Barkhausen, 'Australiens Hölle für Flüchtlinge', *Der Tagesspiegel,* 10 August 2016.

174 H. Davidson, 'Manus Island: MSF denied access to refugees as thousands rally in Australia', *The Guardian*, 26 November 2017, https://www.theguardian.com/australia-news/2017/nov/26/manus-island-msf-denied-access-to-refugees-as-thousands-rally-in-australia (accessed 19 January 2018).

175 'Merkel: Migration aus Afrika ist zentrales Problem',
    Deutsche Welle, 21 June 2016. http://dw.com/p/1JAwu
    (accessed 1 July 2016).
176 W. Grenz et al., *Schiffbruch: Das Versagen der
    europäischen Flüchtlingspolitik*, Munich, Knaur TB, 2015,
    p. 109.
177 'Europäischer Menschengerichtshof untersagt
    Abschiebungen nach Griechenland', *Der Standard*, 21
    January 2011.
178 'Orban lehnt Flüchtlingsquote strikt ab', *Zeit-Online*,
    4 March 2016, http://www.zeit.de/news/2016-03/04/
    international-maas-seehofer-hintertreibt-europa-
    loesung-04065802 (accessed 1 August 2016).
179 S. Luft, *Die Flüchtlingskrise: Ursachen, Konflikte, Folgen*,
    Munich, C. H. Beck, 2016, p. 55.
180 'IOM Applauds Italy's Life Saving Mare Nostrum
    Operation', *International Organization for Migration*,
    31 October 2014, http://www.iom.int/news/
    iom-applauds-italys-life-saving-mare-nostrum-operation-
    not-migrant-pull-factor (accessed 1 August 2016).
181 'EU einig über neuen Grenz- und Küstenschutz',
    Deutsche Welle, 22 June 2016, http://dw.com/p/1JBET
    (accessed 1 August 2016).
182 G. P. Schmitz, 'Überwachung per Eurosur: EU kauft Big-
    Brother-System für das Mittelmeer', *Spiegel-Online*, 10
    October 2013, http://www.spiegel.de/politik/ausland/
    eurosur-ueberwachung-statt-rettung-a-927140.html
    (accessed 19 January 2018).
183 R. Homann, 'Hightech für die Außengrenze', *WDR 5
    Dok 5 – Das Feature* [podcast], 29 May 2016, https://
    podtail.com/podcast/wdr-5-dok-5-das-feature/

hightech-fur-die-aussengrenze-das-ard-radiofe/ (accessed 19 January 2016).

184 G. Gillen, 'Wo beginnt die Festung Europa?' in Anja Reschke (ed.), *Und das ist erst der Anfang: Deutschland und die Flüchtlinge*, Reinbek, Rowohlt Taschenbuch Verlag, 2015, pp. 166–193.

185 D. Bax, 'Der Deal liegt in Trümmern', *Die Tageszeitung*, 19 July 2016, http://www.taz.de/EU-Fluechtlingsabkommen-mit-der-Tuerkei/!5319941 (accessed 1 August 2016).

186 S. Shetty et al., 'Say no to a bad deal with Turkey', *Amnesty International*, 17 March 2016, https://www.amnesty.org/en/latest/news/2016/03/say-no-to-a-bad-deal-with-turkey (accessed 1 August 2016).

187 'A European Union Emergency Trust Fund for Africa', *European Commission*, 12 November 2015, http://europa.eu/rapid/press-release_MEMO-15-6056_en.htm (accessed 15 August 2016).

188 B. Wesel, 'Zuckerbrot und Peitsche in der Flüchtlingspolitik', *Deutsche Welle*, 7 June 2016, http://dw.com/p/1J29x (accessed 1 August 2016).

189 'Declaration of the Ministerial Conference of the Khartoum Process', *2014 Italian Presidency of the Council of the European Union*, http://italia2014.eu/media/3785/declaration-of-the-ministerial-conference-of-the-khartoum-process.pdf (accessed 1 August 2016).

190 K. Matthaei, 'Europas fragwürdige Kooperation mit Afrikas Regimen', *Deutsche Welle*, 4 September 2015, http://dw.com/p/1GRJV (accessed 1 August 2016).

191 L. Feuerbach, 'Ein Bericht aus der Hölle', *Frankfurter Allgemeine Sonntagszeitung*, 11 October 2015.

192 World Development Index 2016, *United Nations Development Programme*, http://report.hdr.undp.org/ (accessed 19 January 2018).

193 A. Kriesch and J.P. Scholz, 'Das lukrative Geschäft mit Afrikas Migrantinnen', *Deutsche Welle*, 16 March 2016, http://dw.com/p/1IBaS (accessed 15 August 2016).

194 F. Schaap, 'Diese Männer werden wahrscheinlich sterben', *Die Zeit*, no. 34, 11 August 2016.

195 'Niger – Mehr Geld für Migrationseindämmung nötig', *Reuters*, 17 June 2016, http://de.reuters.com/article/europa-fl-chtlinge-niger-idDEKCN0Z31I1 (accessed 17 August 2016).

196 Grenz et al., op. cit., pp. 92f.

197 Matthaei, op. cit.

198 'Reject dangerous migration response plan, more than 100 NGOs tell EU leaders', *Amnesty International*, 27 June 2016, https://www.amnesty.org/en/latest/news/2016/06/ngo-joint-statement-migration-eu (accessed 19 January 2018).

199 See 'Germany 2016/2017', *Amnesty International*, https://www.amnesty.org/en/countries/europe-and-central-asia/germany/report-germany (accessed 19 January 2018).

200 Cf. P. Gaibazzi, 'Die Reisefreiheit der anderen', *Le Monde Diplomatique*, 13 December 2013.

201 'Transforming our world: the 2030 Agenda for Sustainable Development', *General Assembly of the United Nations*, 21 October 2015, http://www.un.org/ga/search/view_doc.asp?symbol=A/RES/70/1&Lang=E (accessed 19 January 2018).

202 Ibid.

203 J. Grossarth, 'Der Staat streicht die meisten Agrar-
     Subventionen ein', *Faz.net*, 31 May 2015, http://
     www.faz.net/aktuell/wirtschaft/wirtschaftspolitik/
     empfaengerliste-veroeffentlicht-der-staat-streicht-die-
     meisten-agrar-subventionen-ein-13622450.html (accessed
     1 August 2016).
204 'Billigfleisch für Afrika', *Zeit-Online*, 20 January 2015,
     http://www.zeit.de/wirtschaft/2015-01/exporte-
     gefluegel-afrika (accessed 1 August 2016).
205 A. Paasch, 'Freihandel macht hungrig', *Le Monde
     Diplomatique*, 13 January 2012.
206 M. Auvillain and S. Liberti, 'Tomatensoße für Ghana', *Le
     Monde Diplomatique*, 7 August 2014.
207 M. Krupa and C. Lobenstein, 'Ein Mann pflückt gegen
     Europa', *Die Zeit,* no. 51, 17 December 2015.
208 A. Lorenz, 'Streit über EU-Handelsabkommen mit
     Ostafrika', *EURACTIV.de*, 16 August 2016, http://www.
     euractiv.de/section/entwicklungspolitik/news/streit-
     ueber-eu-handelsabkommen-mit-ostafrika (accessed 20
     August 2016).
209 Krupa and Lobenstein, op. cit.
210 On the fisheries policy of the EU and Africa, see
     J. S. Mora, 'Europas Raubzüge zur See', *Le Monde
     Diplomatique*, 11 January 2013.
211 J. Vidal, 'Seven steps to prevent the collapse of west
     Africa's fishing grounds', *The Guardian*, 2 April 2012,
     https://www.theguardian.com/global-development/
     poverty-matters/2012/apr/02/steps-prevent-collapse-
     west-africa-fishing (accessed 1 August 2016).
212 For an overview of the EU's fisheries agreements with
     individual African countries, see 'Bilateral agreements
     with countries outside the EU', *European Commission*,

https://ec.europa.eu/fisheries/cfp/international/
agreements (accessed 1 August 2016).

213 Vidal, op. cit.
214 Mora, op. cit.
215 'Geographical Distribution of Financial Flows to
Developing Countries 2017', OECD Publishing, http://
www.keepeek.com/Digital-Asset-Management/oecd/
development/geographical-distribution-of-financial-
flows-to-developing-countries-2017_fin_flows_dev-2017-
en-fr#page76 (accessed 19 January 2018).
216 For a brief overview of the different positions, see B.
Grill, 'Wofür das Ganze?', *Die Zeit,* no. 3, 11 January
2007.
217 Perry, op. cit., pp. 31f.
218 Ibid., pp. 44f.
219 W. Easterly, *The White Man's Burden*, Oxford, Oxford
University Press, 2007. See also 'Five minutes with
Angus Deaton (Part 2)', *London School of Economics*, 12
December 2013, http://blogs.lse.ac.uk/politicsandpolicy/
five-minutes-with-angus-deaton-part-2 (accessed 1
August 2016).
220 A. Kabou, *Et si l'Afrique refusait le développement?*, Paris,
L'Harmattan, 1991.
221 J. Shikwati, 'Fehlentwicklungshilfe', Internationale
Politik, 61, no. 4, 2006.
222 V. Seitz, *Afrika wird armregiert oder Wie man Afrika
wirklich helfen kann*, Munich, Deutscher Taschenbuch
Verlag, 2009, pp. 168–170.
223 A. Kriesch, 'Utopie oder Vision? Entwicklungsminister
Müller fordert Marshallplan für Afrika', *Deutsche Welle*,
12 August 2016, http://dw.com/p/1Jh6f (accessed 15
August 2015).

224 P. Collier, 'African Growth: Why a "Big Push"?', *Journal of African Economies*, vol. 15, 2006, suppl. 2, pp. 188–211.

225 S. Mair, 'Flüchtlinge aus Afrika', *SWP-Aktuell*, no. 33, August 2004, pp. 1–4.

226 T. Furster and P. Fischer, 'Nobelpreisträger und Kritiker der Entwicklungshilfe: "Das ist nichts anderes als Kolonialismus"', *NZZ-Online*, 16 June 2016, http://www.nzz.ch/wirtschaft/wirtschaftspolitik/angus-deaton-im-interview-das-ist-nichts-anderes-als-kolonialismus-ld.89298 (accessed 1 August 2016).

227 S. Ellis, 'Afrikanische Ansichten', *Le Monde Diplomatique,* 8 March 2013.

228 L. Sanusi, 'Africa Must Get Real About Chinese Ties', *The Financial Times*, 11 March 2013, http://www.ft.com/cms/s/0/562692b0-898c-11e2-ad3f-00144feabdc0.html (accessed 1 August 2016).

229 N. Liebert, 'Zhing-zhong für Afrika', *Le Monde Diplomatique*, 13 March 2009.

230 Cf. J. Dieterich, 'Der neue Erbe von Nelson Mandela', *Tages-Anzeiger*, 3 January 2016; I. Pfaff, 'John Magufuli – der Bulldozer von Tansania', *Süddeutsche-Online*, 26 April 2016, http://www.sueddeutsche.de/politik/tansania-der-bulldozer-1.2967549 (accessed 1 August 2016).

231 See '#WhatWouldMagufuliDo', *Twitter*, https://twitter.com/hashtag/WhatWouldMagufuliDo (accessed 20 August 2016).

ACKNOWLEDGEMENTS

I would first like to thank Anne-Marie Kasper, whose help in furnishing me with a host of documents from libraries and databases was invaluable to me in researching this book.

I also owe a great debt of gratitude to my editor Rainer Wieland, who once again supported me admirably at every stage during the genesis of this project.

In addition, I should like to express my thanks to the many business figures, academics, journalists and political commentators, both African and European, who have shared their insights on current affairs with me in interviews and conversations.

My especial thanks are due to the African students, refugees and migrants who recounted to me the things they have experienced and told me about their hopes for the future.

Asfa-Wossen Asserate